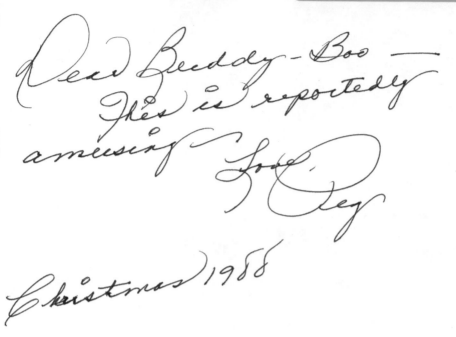

Dear Beddy - Boo —
This is reportedly
amusing. Love, Dey

Christmas, 1988

LEARNING
TO SAIL
THE HARD WAY

LEARNING
TO SAIL
THE HARD WAY

George G. Kirstein

David McKay Company, Inc.
New York

For Frances

Library of Congress Cataloging in Publication Data

Kirstein, George G
Learning to sail the hard way.

1. Sailing.   I. Title
GV811.K57   797.1'24   79-13226
ISBN 0-679-51179-2

1 2 3 4 5 6 7 8 9 10

MANUFACTURED IN THE UNITED STATES OF AMERICA

Contents

Introduction

How many times have all of us heard someone say,
"I haven't ever been able to learn how to do anything
by reading books." Whether the subject under discus-
sion is carpentry, playing chess, backgammon, or
repairing an automobile engine, some people's minds
do not correlate what they read with how they perform. While I do not claim membership in this legion, I
have learned far more from trying to perform manual
tasks on my own than I have either from instructors or
books. Sailing is Exhibit "A" of my self-education. I
have been sailing, racing, or cruising in small boats for
more than fifty years, and if I have learned anything

about what not to do—and I must have learned something because I have survived—it has been by doing it wrong in the first place. So this is not a how-to-do-it book; this is a how-not-to-do-it book. As an instructor in this unfortunate practice, I feel I have few peers. I have ripped sails, dismasted boats, been aground countless times, dragged anchor in nearly every harbor on the eastern seaboard, been lost at night in well-lighted waters, confused in fog, brought up the rear in a multitude of races, quite inadvertently been at sea in storms (including one hurricane), and, in general, made almost every mistake the mind of man can encompass.

Lest this recitation of disaster discourage the reader from continuing further, let me add with a humility which is richly deserved that there are quite a few silver racing trophies in my home, that I have sailed the coast of Nova Scotia three times, sailed my boat to the Caribbean twice and its waters for two years, sailed the Bahamas, Chesapeake Bay, and spent dozens of summers along my home New England coast. I must have learned something because my present boat is as unscathed as the day I bought it. But my education was achieved by learning the hard way.

My house overlooks Long Island Sound at one of America's busiest yachting centers. More than one thousand boats are moored each summer in this harbor. Larchmont, another hub of activity, is only a mile distant; and City Island, Manhasset, and Port Washington, all with large fleets, are less than an hour's sail away. Each spring I watch the drama of beginners courting disaster in fair weather and foul, as they learn how to sail their boats the "hard way." This recurrent spectacle is as predictable as the return of the swallows each spring, and while it is near tragedy for the participants, it is an amusing spectator sport for observers on the shore.

About four times each summer, the distress of these neophytes moves me to intervene by towing them with my 13-foot motorboat to a nearby dock. I used to have a large Newfoundland dog, who enjoyed participating in these "rescues." Newfoundlands, because of their great swimming ability, were used by lifeguards in Canada to carry ropes through the surf to stranded vessels, beached just off shore. While "Skipper's" life was the prosaic lot of a house pet, the blood of his ancestors coursed through his huge body as we sped to aid the disabled mariner. I always figured that being thoroughly licked by this 170-pound, tailwagging monster was sufficient punishment to assure that the beginner would never repeat the same mistake again.

Another motive has spurred my rescue efforts—I had been there myself under similar circumstances. Most of the value of learning the hard way is to get out of the mess yourself. Therefore I select the victims to whom I lend a hand with some care. If they are not in serious trouble—for example, are about to be blown ashore in a gentle wind in a shoal draft boat—I figure they are not in danger and will learn more without assistance. On the other hand, if there is any doubt I help them as others have helped me. I have never once been refused assistance when I needed it, and I hope I have repaid my debt to all those decent people by behaving in like manner.

The great comedians of silent film, Charlie Chaplin, Harold Lloyd, and Buster Keaton, created comedy by simulating disaster absolutely deadpan. Audiences howled with laughter at their misadventures. I can assure the reader the catalogue of disaster embodied in the pages that follow were not funny at the time. Like a good wine, age mellows memory. Most of the lessons learned the hard way seem funny to me now. I can only hope my readers will be amused, and possibly learn something themselves.

1

Kindergarten

We summered in Marblehead when I was a child, and the abundant yachting activity in that busy harbor acted as a magnet on adolescents. I do not recall whether I suggested the type of boat to acquire or whether my father made inquiry from some of his Marblehead neighbors, but the choice of my first vessel was a 13-foot O boat. This little centerboarder with its outboard rudder had been designed by Boston's foremost naval architect, John Alden, as a suitable craft in which children could learn sailing and race against each other. The boats were all built in the Marblehead yard of James Graves, and their sails were made by a single sailmaker. *Rose,* named after my mother, carried the number "32" indicating that thirty-one boats had preceded this one. My hazy recollection is that the boat cost $600. Ordered during Easter vacation, the craft was ready in June of 1925 when school recessed for summer vacation.

She was a beautiful object when I proudly steered her robin's egg blue hull at the end of a towline to the mooring just off our summer residence. But in retrospect, the O boats were miserable little vessels, one of the few failures in the total output of a first-rate naval architect. They were fat, slow and, when the test came, unseaworthy. A severe summer thundersquall in 1928 capsized half the racing fleet and, to everyone's surprise, twelve of them sank. Fortunately no one was drowned, but the incident doomed the O boats to oblivion. They were originally designed to have flotation air tanks of galvanized steel under their seats, but it was customary to remove both the seats and the tanks in order to reduce weight and gain an advantage in racing. Therefore, Alden cannot be held entirely responsible for the high casualty rate which resulted from that squall.

The theory of using the wind for propulsion is simple. Obviously, no wind-driven craft can make progress directly into the eye of the wind; so, if one desires to go in that direction, one *tacks* by sailing 45 degrees off the wind in one direction. Then, by turning the bow through the wind's eye, one sails 45 degrees off it in the other direction. With the exception of the quadrant from which the wind is blowing, a sailboat is free to progress in any other direction merely by adjusting the sails so that they are approximately perpendicular to the wind's flow. The only essential fact required to sail a boat is to locate the exact direction of the wind which is easily ascertainable by observing flags, or smoke plumes.

Simple as they are, it took me weeks to gain even a rudimentary understanding of these fundamentals. The boatbuilder who had produced *Rose* recommended a taciturn New Englander as sailing instructor, and for three sessions two boyhood friends accompanied me in sailing around the harbor under this man's tutelage. He must have explained the simple rules to us, but either we were so delighted with the new sensation of sailing that we paid no attention to his instruction, or we just did not understand what he was talking about. After the three lessons, conducted in typically light summer breezes, we dispensed with the instructor and proceeded on our own.

From the beginning, disaster struck repeatedly. We made every mistake imaginable. We collided with boats peaceably moored and helpless before our onslaught. We hit rocks. We tore sails. We somehow evolved the totally false theory that the tighter we pulled in the sails, the faster we would go. We formed this unwarranted conclusion because we heeled further over when the sails were in tight, and we thought tipping, which was exciting, equated with speed. As a result, we nearly capsized at least a dozen times, and half-swamped the boat on countless occasions.

The prevailing summer winds in Marblehead are light southwest breezes off the land, so that for the most part a tolerant nature did not punish us for the multitude of mistakes we committed. One extremely hot afternoon the wind piped up to a velocity that, in our inexperienced eyes, approached gale force. Prudence dictated that we promptly head for the safety of our mooring before some new and unexpected calamity struck. To repeat the fundamental axiom of sailing,

The author's first "teacher," an Alden O boat, Rose, *sailing in Marblehead Harbor. She was built by Graves, her sails were by Cousen & Pratt, and she was 13' OA. The author owned* Rose *between 1923 and 1925.*

a boat cannot proceed into the eye of the wind. Therefore, if you wish to stop a boat's progress, you merely point the bow into the wind, and, with sails flapping, the vessel will come to a halt within a few yards. If the objective is to pick up a floating object, a mooring buoy, for example, the maneuver calls for positioning the boat a few yards downwind from the target, then pointing the bow directly into the wind's eye, thus being able to retrieve the object as the vessel comes to a halt. One would think that even a bright baby could figure that out. But I didn't. With her bow pointed unwaveringly at the floating buoy, I drove *Rose* dead before that strong wind at maximum speed toward the mooring. As we sped past the floating buoy, one of my loyal crew grabbed it and was nearly pulled overboard. Hercules could not have held that buoy against the momentum of the onrushing *Rose*. As he released the mooring only an instant before dislocating his arms, he yelled, "I can't hold it." Undaunted, I repeated the tactic. By sailing in the now frighteningly strong wind across the harbor and back, I again positioned *Rose* above the buoy and charged full speed at it with exactly the same result.

By this time our antics had attracted spectators. Unfortunate owners of threatened boats moored nearby shouted and gesticulated from the shore. They pantomimed the correct strategy. I failed to understand, and for the third time called on my crew for a display of superhuman strength as we rushed past the floating buoy. Discouraged by two failures, this time my crew did not even try to grab the mooring.

At this point, Bob Thayer, owner of the neighboring O boat, *Surprise,* and racing leader of the class, launched his rowboat and came toward us to offer advice.

"Sail near my boat," Bob yelled, "and then head for your mooring."

As *Surprise* was moored directly downwind from my mooring, when I followed his advice, *Rose* lost her way as she came into the wind and stopped exactly next to the elusive buoy. After we tied up the boat and lowered the flapping sails, Bob came aboard. He was considerably older than we, and would enter college as a freshman the next fall. He and his older brother Dick had sailed *Surprise* to an almost unbroken string of victories in O boat racing. For half an hour on that windy afternoon, Bob instructed us in the theory of sailing. The blinders fell from our eyes. The reasons for our multitude of catastrophes were suddenly explained. It was like finally mastering the trick of balancing a bicycle after repeated failures, falls, and collisions.

Fifty years have elapsed since that memorable afternoon. Heaven knows how many books from primers for beginners to learned treatises on the aerodynamics of sails have been published in that interlude. Nevertheless, as an expert witness I can attest that the most frequent problem that today's beginners face is failure to understand that it is impossible to sail a boat into the eye of the wind. Sails aflutter, frequently progressing backward toward a rocky shore, the neophyte persists in pointing his boat in the direction he wishes to go. Recently I felt sorry enough for a lone Sunfish sailor who was drifting backward onto a particularly forbidding sea wall to yell at him, "You can's sail it into the wind. Point it toward me and pull in the sail." The tiny craft gathered way on the first leg of a tack. As he passed, he yelled, "Thanks." I offered one more piece of advice. "Turn it at right angles to the way you are going now, and keep the sail in." He followed directions, and waved appreciation. He had learned to tack the hard way.

While Bob's lecture taught us how to stop the boat and how to tack, we still did not thoroughly understand that there are two ways a boat can pass through the wind's eye. The first—putting its bow into the wind—we mastered. We did not quite realize that bringing the stern around through the wind had an entirely different effect. But we learned the hard way. We had mastered the proposition that pulling the sails in tight did not increase speed. Now when we ran before the wind the boom and sail were out at right angles to the hull. Running before the wind is deceptive in that the speed of the vessel is subtracted from the true speed of the wind. Thus if *Rose* were sailing at five knots before a fifteen-knot wind, the apparent wind would have been only a moderate ten-knot force.

It was a beautiful afternoon, with a cloudless sky and a fine breeze. *Rose* was bound out of the harbor with her happy crew in swimming trunks, running before the southwest wind with boom and sail all the way out. Disaster! Either the wind shifted a few points or my steering wavered. The boom rocketed from all the way out on one side to all the way out on the other. But the sail did not follow. The edge of the canvas had caught on the mast's steel spreader that kept the wire rigging taut. When the boom slammed over, the sail ripped straight across and was flopping in two pieces. The boom, without the support of the sail, fell into the sea, its ropes entangled in the rudder. The only reason no one had been hurt was we were all lying on the cockpit bottom.

Somehow we cleared up the mess and retrieved our mooring with just the jib furnishing power. A rival O boat skipper who had witnessed this latest humiliation said, as we went ashore, "Wow, that wasn't just a jibe. That was a 'Chinese' jibe."

Call it what you will—"Chinese," "accidental," or "inadvertent"—we learned to be a lot more careful while running before the wind. A computer would have difficulty in totalling the number of accidental jibes I have perpetrated since that day. Running down following seas makes accurate steering difficult, but at least the sail was never out its full limit nor were the results of subsequent jibes as disastrous. The correct tactic if your course calls for a straight downwind run is to tie the boom down in such a way that it can't swing across in devastating fashion. Better still is to tack downwind. Sail the boat with the wind behind you, but slightly over one corner of the stern. Halfway to your destination, jibe by pulling in the main and change course. Then let it out gently on the other side.

All of these disheartening lessons had taken perhaps a month. At least, we had learned that the wind makes boats go, can stop them, and, if not respected, can damage them. There was much more to learn. One afternoon, I was privileged to listen in on a conversation between Bob Thayer and his brother and coskipper, Dick, when they were analyzing why they had come in second in a race rather than leading the fleet as usual.

"We should have stood over toward Cat Island on that first tack," Dick said. "With the tide ebbing and with wind southwest, it was a mistake to stand in for the shore."

"Do you mean to say that for each wind direction, depending on the tide, there is a preferred course to sail?" I asked.

"Of course," Dick replied. "Also the wind speed makes a difference. If it's blowing hard enough, the stronger wind off the land will offset the advantage of the stronger current off the shore. Of course, if the wind is northwest, the whole situation changes."

With an abyss of new ignorance opening before me, I asked, "How can you ever learn all the possible combinations of wind and tide when there are half a dozen courses that we race around?"

"Oh, that's not so hard," Dick said. "What's tough is anticipating shifts in the wind so, that regardless of tide, you will be in the right place to take advantage of the shift."

I was bedazzled by this huge new vista, but before the summer was over much more was to come: cloud formations that betrayed shifting winds, weather maps published in the daily papers, the color of sunsets, the gathering haze that presages a wind shift to the southwest, the knowledge that northwest winds are gusty near the shore, that southeast winds tend to have fewer flaws than others, and many other natural phenomena. We learned a lot about the winds that summer, their force, their power, their direction, but the hardest lesson we learned was that after all our experience, we knew almost nothing. Fifty years have elapsed, and that truth is abiding.

2

The Harsh Lessons of Racing

Bob Thayer had added one piece of advice to his lecture: "You ought to begin racing. You'll learn more about sailing by racing than any other way. We have a junior yacht club for members under seventeen, and I'll put up your name. But start racing and don't be scared of being last."

The following Saturday, we entered *Rose* in her first race. I had no clear idea of racing tactics, rules for the right of way, or even starting procedures, so we adopted a very simple strategy—to follow Bob Thayer closely in his *Surprise*. We knew that we could not win by following a leader, but we calculated that coming in

10

second right behind *Surprise* would not be a bad position particularly in view of the fact that some twenty-five other O boats were racing that afternoon. It was a brilliant strategy, albeit a modest one, but one important flaw developed. We could not stay close enough to *Surprise* even to be able to imitate her. From the start she pulled away from us at such a rate that halfway around the course she was almost out of sight. So, incidentally, were most of the other twenty-five competitors. We finished last, not just last, but ignominiously last, trailing the fleet by half a mile over a three mile course. We were behind the next to last boat by well over two hundred yards.

Knowing that we could only improve, we persisted. Every Wednesday, Saturday and Sunday afternoon when races were conducted for the O boats, *Rose* was out racing. And every single afternoon we finished last. As I recall it, there was finally one, memorable afternoon when an unfortunate competitor tore a sail and our finishing position thus improved to next to last.

Through our persistence, we learned certain truths about sailboat racing which apply to all of the many fleets I subsequently raced with, and perhaps to all of life's contests as well. The O boat fleet divided into three recognizable divisions. At the top were two winners, the Thayer brothers in *Surprise,* and Arthur Schuman, who many years later became the sailing instructor at the United States Naval Academy. It was a rare event when the winner's gun greeted any boat other than one of those two. Below them in the class standings, there were perhaps fifteen boats whose positions shuffled from race to race, but only once or twice each season did one of these emerge as a winner, although they were never at the bottom of the fleet.

Finally there were the tailenders, perhaps five boats in all, skippered by those just learning to sail, or with no aptitude for the sport. *Rose* was the tailendest of the tailenders.

Notwithstanding this disheartening introduction to racing, my enthusiasm remained undiminished. Not only the aesthetic pleasures of observing sea and sky punctuated by the white sails and graceful hulls of the racing fleet that gratified me. My main enjoyment came from the responsibility of command, from my newly found right to determine courses of action without adult interference, from the first discovery of the joys of nonsupervised freedom. During the next school year, I interspersed my mandatory studies of Latin, French, and geometry with an intensive elective, self-administered course in yacht racing tactics. I memorized the basic rules controlling right of way. I read essays with titles like "How to Start a Race," "Rounding Marks to Gain Advantage," and "When to Set the Spinnaker." I learned so much I had not known before that by the time the second summer season of sailing opened, I was confident that I had become an accomplished sailor. What folly at fifteen or fifty to believe the sea and the wind disclose their secrets so easily.

With the last summer's practical experience behind us and armed with the new knowledge I generously shared with my two-man crew, we entered the first race of the new season with high hopes of finishing right behind the unbeatable Bob Thayer. We were last. We were last in the next two races as well. I asked Bob what we were doing wrong. He said, "I didn't pay much attention to your boat, but it looked to me as if the jib stay was sagging. Also the luff of your mainsail was wrinkled which means the tension along the boom may have been slack." He went on, "The way to tune up a boat is to get someone in the class to sail with you in the same wind and water. Change the tension on the stays, try the sails with different settings, and adjust things until the boat is doing her best."

I persuaded another one of the tailenders to sail with us, and for a week our two boats sailed around the harbor, always on the same course, with the crews making adjustments in the rake of the masts, the set of the sails, the positions of centerboards and rudders. For the first time in the thrice weekly races, a few boats were behind us at the finish line.

As O boats were very small, the distribution of weight had a profound effect on their individual sailing qualities. The little vessels had several dozen bars of lead for inside ballast under the floor boards in their cockpits. How these bars were placed made a difference. Of even more importance was the placement of the crew for different points of sailing and for different wind speeds. For example, the boats ran before light winds faster when their bows were high and their sterns low in the water. Therefore, it seemed advantageous for all three of us to huddle in the very rear of the cockpit once we had rounded the final mark and were headed for the finish line. But the force of stronger winds tended to lift the bow so the proper position of the crew was near the middle of the boat. The only way to ascertain whether weight placement was advantageous or not was to shift around while racing near another boat to see whether *Rose* gained or lost by the new distribution. This was by no means a scientific method for the set of sails, the way the boat was steered, and the effect of our nearby competition on the wind were all variables. We learned painfully that the techniques of competitive sailing were not as simple as we had confidently believed so short a time ago.

Our standings in racing improved a little over the course of the summer. We were rarely last toward the end, but we certainly did not move up to join that middle section of the fleet which finished right behind the winners. With all our new knowledge and improved skills, we began to suspect that our poor showing was due to defects inherent in *Rose.* Even when the same builder constructs a whole fleet to a single design and all sails are made by the same loft, one boat can be a clunker. In certain championship races when boats are exchanged to visiting skippers for each race, the same boat will finish last every time regardless of who sails her. I will never know whether our poor results were to any degree *Rose's* fault. The only way to have tested this theory would have been to exchange boats with Arthur Schuman and Bob Thayer for a number of races to see whether they could achieve better results. With class championships being decided between these two toward the summer's end, any exchange program was unthinkable. So without any real proof that the blame lay in some flaw in the boat, the decision was made to sell *Rose,* thus removing what may have been a convenient alibi for our consistently poor showing.

After this second season, the summer of 1926, a number of people who had learned sailing as children in the ungainly little O boats had grown to college age and wanted to graduate to heavier, more seaworthy vessels that presented more challenge for their skills. In addition, a number of adults with teen-age children desired boats large enough to permit summer racing to be a family affair. A group of prospective owners commissioned John Alden to design the new class, and

Rose II, *a Triangle Class sloop, racing off Marblehead. George Kirstein's second "teacher" was 18 feet on the waterline, 25 feet overall. She was built by Graves, with sails by Cousen & Pratt. The author owned her from 1926 to 1928.*

this time he created a masterpiece—a fast, seaworthy, safe and comfortable day sailer. Again Graves was awarded the contract to build some twenty identical vessels, and a single Boston sailmaker produced all the sails for the new fleet. Because a triangle, the class symbol, was sewn on each mainsail just below the racing number, the new fleet was called the Triangle Class; and some forty years after their introduction a few of these boats are still racing in various New England harbors. *Rose II* was the thirteenth produced so she carried that traditionally unlucky number on her sail, but it proved not to be unlucky for us.

That June afternoon when we sailed her away from her builder's yard she seemed awesomely large because we had never handled a craft larger than our little 13-foot O boat. *Rose II* was eighteen-feet long on the waterline and with her long graceful overhangs at both bow and stern, she measured twenty-five feet overall. Instead of the centerboard which had cluttered up the O boat's cockpit, *Rose II* had a keel which gave her stability as well as momentum when she plowed into the long sea swells that characterize much of Marblehead's summer weather pattern. Best of all, she had a cabin; at least if you were sixteen years old, you could flatter the structure by calling it a cabin. By dropping to hands and knees, we could enter the three-foot high structure which was perhaps eight feet long. On each side of this cabin was a slatted wooden bench, designed primarily to store spare sails and equipment, but in our eyes these benches were berths, and the possibility of overnight cruising opened before us.

Racing in this class was a new and heady experience. Instead of the short courses we had sailed in the O boats, usually set out in protected harbor waters, the Triangles raced over six to eight mile courses in the open ocean. Because all the boats were new, no skipper had the advantage of previous experience with them. Finally, if there was a "clunker" in the fleet, and I do not recall that there was, *Rose II* was certainly not it. We deserted for all time the tailender group, and even occasionally won a completely useless silver-plated cigarette box, ash tray, cream pitcher, or orange juice squeezer with *Rose II*'s name engraved on it as a trophy for coming in near the top of the fleet. Not that the winner's cannon constantly deafened us; indeed, I do not recall winning a single race, for the Thayer brothers and Arthur Schuman dominated the new class as they had in the O boats. However, occasional lucky wind shifts or races where the usual leaders were absent sometimes furnished us with the satisfaction of seeing most of the fleet behind us.

Our improved status might have given us an unwarranted self-confidence had it not been for the publication that year of a book by a German aerodynamics expert. *Yacht Racing: The Aerodynamics of Sails and Racing Tactics* by Dr. Manfred Curry disclosed vast new areas of abysmal ignorance. Even today more than forty-five years later as I thumb through the water-stained, dogeared pages of this treatise, I am impressed with the author's ingenuity; and when the book first appeared, it was revolutionary. We discovered the secrets of the "safe leeward position," and the advantages under certain conditions of "tacking downwind," as well as the horrors of the "hopeless position," one that we had occupied all too many times in the past without understanding why we fell further and further behind. By the use of wind tunnels and towing tanks, Curry had examined the distortions in both wind and water caused by a boat's progress. He studied the friction of different shaped hulls and

17

different weight sails, and he recommended racing tactics based on his research. We studied that book with the devotion a monk gives to the scriptures and began to comprehend the limitless depths of our ignorance.

Armed with this new theoretical knowledge, the second summer we raced *Rose II* we improved our position still more. Now, we finished in that middle part of the fleet which occasionally challenged the leaders. My small assortment of silver ash trays and plated mugs that rewarded good performance grew. At the end of that summer, college loomed ahead, and after college early jobs that offered little time for sailing. Some eight years elapsed before I again was at the tiller of a boat as the cannon signalled the start of a race.

Now my command was a 30-foot stubby cruising boat, and the race was not around the buoys but a fifty-mile event. It started in Greenwich with the turning point at Stratford Shoal Lighthouse in the middle of Long Island Sound, and to complicate matters it started at night. Pilotage presented new problems. So long as we sailed in daytime with the land in sight, we could keep track of where we were. *Tarheel,* of course, had a compass which when needed could be fitted into a bracket in the cockpit, but the few times we used it gave us little confidence that it pointed truly to the north. Before the race was three hours old, we were completely lost. In the middle of the night, we found ourselves mysteriously surrounded by land. It was as if we had somehow sailed into a pond without knowing it, and could find no way out. We seemed to be surrounded by lights, none of which helped us in locating our position. There was nothing to do except anchor and wait for dawn to disclose the dangers that

Kirstein's third "teacher," Tarheel, *at her mooring in Rye, New York. Owned from 1935 to 1938,* Tarheel *was a gaff-rigged auxiliary sloop, 25' WL, 30' OA. She was designed and built by Casey of Fairhaven, Massachusetts. Her sails were by Manchester and she had a 2-cylinder Kermath engine.*

lay in every direction. When the sun came up, we found we were deep inside the recesses of Smithtown Bay, and some of the lights we had mistaken as being on shore had been on vessels passing in the sound. We turned on the engine and shamefacedly admitted to the race committee that we had been forced to withdraw due to "navigational error."

The following summer, somewhat more experienced in keeping track of our position, we determined to erase the shame of our ignominious beginning to long distance racing by again entering the same annual race. I recruited my full experienced crew of three men plus Jacquette, who later became my wife. *Tarheel* had a spinnaker that required two men to set, and, in addition, her old-fashioned gaff rig with its heavy spars required male strength to manipulate. As she had no winches, all sails had to be trimmed by brute strength without mechanical help. Furthermore, in any kind of a breeze, she carried such a strong weather helm that her tiller pulled like an unruly mule. Four men and a cook were really the minimum she required for efficient handling in an overnight race of fifty miles.

The evening before the race Jackie, John, one of the prospective crew, and I took the boat over to Greenwich and anchored in the harbor. The next morning John and I caught an early commuter train to the city. Jackie, who worked a five-day week, stayed aboard. Before we departed, I told her that the time handicap assigned to us by the race committee seemed altogether too small. I instructed her to remind the committee when they came to remeasure and inspect the boat that we had an old-fashioned rig and that there must be a mistake somewhere in their computation.

John and I returned from the city in the late

afternoon with the disquieting information that two of our crew were unable to make the race. The yacht club launch ferried us out to *Tarheel*. As we approached we saw that the regatta committee's power boat was just leaving after their measurement and inspection visit. As we climbed aboard, Jackie greeted us. We had become used to what she referred to as her "sunbathing uniform," but the regatta committee must have been dazzled. The narrow scarf she had around her upper body revealed more than it hid, and what kept the scant bikini bottom in place was a mysterious secret. There were a dozen empty beer bottles in the cockpit.

"What in the world is going on?" I asked.

"I've just had a lovely talk with the regatta committee," she explained in a somewhat slurred voice. "You were right. They didn't give us a big enough handicap. They said something about the beam measurement. Anyway, they just added eighteen more minutes to the time the other boats have to give us."

"Beam measurement, indeed," I said. "My God, girl, have you no shame? Go put some clothes on."

She laughed. "You know they stayed here nearly an hour remeasuring, and it only took them a few minutes on the other boats."

"I can believe it," I said.

We went ashore for the prerace banquet at the yacht club, and when it was time to return to *Tarheel* to prepare for the start, I realized I had imbibed too much and eaten too well. As the yacht club launch approached our boat and the three of us prepared to clamber aboard, one of the other contestants asked, "Kind of shorthanded, aren't you?"

I said, "We sure are." Pointing to Jackie, I went on, "And she's absolutely useless."

An immediate clamor went up in the launch.

"We have a spare berth on *Dog Star*."

"We need a cook on *Altair*."

"If they don't want you, *Gray Gull* could surely use you."

"I didn't mean it, Jackie," I told her. "I was only teasing. We really need you." And it turned out we did.

The wind was blowing hard out of the east when we started from the searchlight beam from the committee boat that marked the starting line. Stratford Shoal lay twenty-five miles due east of us in the very eye of the wind. *Tarheel* lay over on her side, deck awash, pulling on her tiller with shoulder-wrenching force. She threw back sheets of spray as she tacked into the wind at her best speed. I was sick. I became sicker as the hours passed. Whether it was caused by overindulgence at the banquet, exhaustion from a week's hard work, the violent motion of *Tarheel* as she slammed into the breaking waves, or a combination of all of these, I do not know. But it was I, not Jackie, who was useless; I didn't even have the strength to spell John at the straining tiller.

Keeping in mind our "navigational error" of the year before, I told John to tack for forty minutes in one direction, then come about, and tack for an equal period the other way. As Stratford Shoal is in mid-Sound and shows a powerful light, I reasoned we would be bound to find it if we tacked down the middle of the course. No factor other than the desire not to get lost again influenced my decision to adopt this tactic, but, by chance, it happened to be exactly the right thing to do. The tide was ebbing, favoring our progress, and it ran faster in the middle of the Sound than near the edges. The strong tide flowing against

22

Tarheel *alongside a dock in 1935.*

the east wind kicked up steep, cresting waves. *Tarheel* threw back a deluge of spray as she plowed into them. It was a miserable, cold, wet night. About six hours after the start and just before dawn, we came up to the lighthouse and rounded for the run back. With the pressure off the tiller now that we had stopped tacking, Jackie had the strength to steer while John and I set the spinnaker. As the sun came up, we saw that there were very few larger boats ahead of us, but the main body of the fleet was astern. Around nine-thirty we crossed the finish line, and the ordeal was over. The committee blew a whistle as we finished, and some of the members waved. I am sure their greeting was directed at their hostess of the previous afternoon and not at her exhausted shipmates. In any case, between John's tireless efforts at the tiller and Jackie's success in enlarging our handicap, we achieved third position in the race. At least we had erased the disgrace of the "navigational error."

We did not race *Tarheel* again. We knew that no matter how persuasive Jackie's costumes might be, regatta committees are not in the habit of enlarging handicaps. And *Tarheel* was ungainly and slow. After Jacquette and I were married, we bought a larger boat, the 36-foot Alden cutter again named *Rose*. As I was savoring my first executive responsibilities in business, we had only weekends to sail. We entered a good many of the overnight races of fifty to seventy-five miles which were conducted virtually every weekend on Long Island Sound. No longer the tailenders of Marblehead days, we usually finished in the upper quarter of the fleet, and occasionally the welcome crack of the winner's gun greeted our return to the finish line.

The sweetest victory we ever enjoyed in *Rose* was

not in a distance, but in an eight-mile afternoon race around the buoys, reminiscent of Marblehead. There were a number of boats in the race, but our only real competitor was *Murrelet,* a perfectly lovely new sloop, which had just joined the fleet. *Rose,* a cutter with two foresails rather than the conventional large genoa, was awkward to tack. Each time we came about, the jib topsail had to be cast off and winched in on the other side. In addition, *Rose* steered with a wheel which slowed her movements in going through the eye of the wind. *Murrelet* had a genoa which trimmed quickly and a tiller that added to her liveliness. At the last mark of this particular race, *Rose* was ahead by perhaps twenty yards, but as we tacked for the finish line *Murrelet,* a faster boat, overtook us. When she gained the lead, we tried to split tacks. Each time *Murrelet* tacked, we tried the other direction. Each time we lost ground, and each time she tacked on top of us. Her lead widened. The only possible tactic if you are behind on a tack is to try to get away from the other boat's cover. It doesn't matter when you face defeat whether you will be beaten by one minute or by half an hour. We kept tacking and losing ground. As we approached the finish line, *Murrelet* let us go our own way as she proceeded on a straight course to victory. But it was not to be. We picked up a private gust of wind on our lonely course, then the wind let us just fetch the finish line. Now *Murrelet* was also heading for the line on the other tack. It was a collision course, but *Rose* held the right of way. *Murrelet* was forced to tack under us as we sped to the finish line. The cannon on the committee boat signalled our passage. Two seconds later, we heard the whistle that indicated *Murrelet* had finished. *Murrelet*'s skipper waved over to us in the congratulatory salute of a good loser. He had learned the "hard way" to never let even a slower boat split tacks when you are ahead.

Racing in unfamiliar waters raises unique problems. In the two years that I kept my 40-foot, fiberglass yawl, *Shag,* in the Virgin Islands, I raced a number of times. We never did well, either because I sailed the boat badly or because my competitors had some local knowledge of wind and current that I did not possess. As it was difficult for me to admit that after all these years my sailing skills were at fault, I decided to recruit a crew of local experts for the annual Fourth of July race of some forty miles circumnavigating St. Thomas. The commodore of my yacht club agreed to act as alternate helmsman, and the commanding officer of the Coast Guard district volunteered to be navigator. Two tackles on the Brown's football team who were doing manual labor in the islands to prepare for the fall season were recruited to man the winches.

The trade winds make the finest sailing I have ever enjoyed, and the Fourth of July was bright with the subtropical sun and the usual wind of twelve to fifteen knots from the east. The other boats seemed gun-shy at the start and we crossed the line first. We tacked the nine miles up to the eastern end of the island, and the commodore took over at the helm. He snaked through a patch of coral that I had always believed was impossible to navigate, and we squared away for the long run down the northern side of the island.

"Stay well out from the shore," the commodore advised. "The wind eddys around those mountains. A straight line is not the shortest way to the other end."

We were still first in the fleet, despite the presence of larger boats, as we rounded the western end of the island and began the tack back to the start.

"Kiss the beach like it was your mother," advised

the Commodore. The Coast Guard officer assured us the water would hold right up to the shore.

We short-tacked up the beach, with the two football players, drenched with sweat, pulling the big 800-foot genoa around every three or four minutes.

I did not take any barnacles off of the shore line, but if those pestiferous shellfish have any reactions, I must have given them nervous breakdowns with my proximity. As we crossed the finish line in beautiful Charlotte Amalie harbor, the cannon on the committee boat welcomed us home.

"I love to hear those guns," I said.

But the credit for *Shag*'s winning final race was not mine. The local knowledge of experienced yachtsmen had taught me the hard way where the fault lay in my previous losing efforts.

3

Cruising Is (Sometimes, Often, Always) Fun

To visit distant ports, to escape the traffic jams and gasoline fumes of crowded highways, to sail under cloudless skies, to sleep under the starlit canopy of heaven, that is what we imagined cruising to be as we prepared *Rose II,* my 18-foot racing boat for our first adventure into the unknown. Only idiots, dwarfs, or teen-agers would have found the Triangles suitable for cruising, for they had neither headroom, toilet facilities, stoves nor accommodations for food storage. They had no water tanks, bedding, nor any of the other features which are generally thought necessary for living afloat.

Nevertheless, we enrolled in the annual junior yacht club cruise the very first summer we sailed *Rose II*. Each year, as part of the training program, a three-day cruise was conducted under the guidance of at least one larger boat, manned by adults, usually the parents of a participating member. In late July, we assembled with the rest of the fleet, a total of seven boats in all, just outside Marblehead harbor.

We again discovered how much we did not know. In the O boats we had never been forced to use a compass because, as trailers in the class, other boats always led us to the designated turning marks. If fog hung heavy, the races in the small boats were either cancelled or confined to the familiar waters of the harbor. Therefore, we knew nothing of the use of charts, or compass variation or deviation, of the use of dividers, or parallel rules, or indeed of any aspect of pilotage in strange waters. Nor had we used navigation lights for night sailing nor even an anchor.

The first leg of the cruise was a run to Gloucester harbor some nine miles from Marblehead. As in all yacht club cruises, the boats raced against each other between ports, and the difference in the size and speed of boats was equalized by some handicap system (which none of us understood) devised by our elders. But the racing was insignificant compared to the adventure of sailing into strange and unexplored waters. In the late afternoon, at the conclusion of the race, the fleet of seven boats was towed through the

Annisquam Canal by the accompanying senior boat. This aspect of the voyage was a revelation. Drawbridges lifted as if by magic while impatient motorists honked at the little procession. The winding, confined waters of the narrow canal would have been impossible to negotiate without the power of the senior boat's engine, and we viewed with awe the boats going through in the opposite direction which avoided collision with us only by inches. The Annisquam Yacht Club assigned moorings at the far end of the canal, so, fortunately we were not required to use the unfamiliar anchor on that initial night.

For the first time, we slept on *Rose II.* We had brought blankets, but the "berths" had no mattresses. We used life preservers as pillows, and after drawing lots my crew occupied the two favored positions, while I slept on the deck between the berths. There was not enough headroom to sit wholly upright without banging your head, but to the young, engaged in adventure, comfort takes a low priority. Early the next morning, the small fleet started its major run, a 25-mile course, to Kittery, Maine. What images Maine held for us: rugged rocks with virgin spruce growing to the water's edge, lobster fishermen, white church steeples, and countless islets. Unfortunately for our dreams of beauty, Kittery, which is barely within Maine's boundary, is the ugly little bight just across the filthy Piscatagua River from the industrial city of Portsmouth, New Hampshire. We anchored near our accompanying schooner, and it was fortunate for us that the senior skipper yelled over to us to let out more anchor line. He was not satisfied until we had released all the 150 feet of line with which the anchor was equipped and *Rose II* stayed in a constant position relative to the other boats. We had believed it was the weight of the anchor that held the boat in place, but our tutor explained the truth to us—that what really held the boat was the anchor flukes biting into the mud bottom.

That night and all the next day it rained. The fog came in and the wind increased. It was miserable. The three of us sat huddled in *Rose II*'s cabin and sang every song we could remember. Occasionally we ate one of the stale sandwiches we had brought along. We took turns telling stories. We slept. The weather forced the postponement of our planned return to Marblehead. After the day dragged to its close, a severe thunderstorm during the night cleared the air. On the fourth day of the cruise, in sparkling weather, with a strong northwest wind at our backs, we raced back around Cape Ann the thirty-five miles to Marblehead. Cruising, we decided, could be fun, but only if the weather was good.

Seven years elapsed between the sale of *Rose II* and the acquisition of *Tarheel*. The Great Depression filled those years, and I ceased being a student, blessed with long summer vacations but became a man whose opportunities to be on the sea were limited to weekends and the short summer vacations granted to all employes of large corporations. Because my experience with cruising was limited to the episode on *Rose II* and because the waters near New York City were entirely unfamiliar, I decided to charter, rather than to buy. I sought a small vessel, not too much larger than *Rose II*, but capable of extending cruising along the waters of Long Island Sound and its vicinity. Inquiries of a yacht broker disclosed that *Tarheel* was available for charter, and she satisfied my requirements.

Tarheel was no beauty. Her rig included the old-fashioned gaff mainsail, although she had been built in

1926 when the more modern marconi rig was already popular. Major Casey had built her at his Fairhaven, Massachusetts yard, and when the ponderous major supervised the building of a boat, she was well and truly made. She was thirty feet on deck, twenty-five feet on the waterline, nearly nine feet wide at her broadest point, and her keel extended five feet below the surface. She had a bowsprit sticking some five feet out ahead of her hull to enable her to carry a large jib (125 square feet). For her size, she had a high deckhouse which gave her an ungainly and rather top-heavy look, but it permitted six feet, one inch of head room throughout her main cabin, which made up in comfort what she sacrificed in appearance.

The engine was set just astern of the steps leading from the cockpit down into the main cabin. No bulkhead separated the machinery from the living quarters so the engine was an ever-present and fre-quently temperamental shipmate. It was a heavy-duty 2 cylinder, 10 hp Kermath, as simple a piece of propulsion machinery as could be devised. Once started, the motor roared along uninterruptedly, ne-cessitating the raising of voices to just below a scream. But starting it, there was the rub. One never had to trace the cause of its reluctance to either the battery or the self-starter; it had neither. The procedure for starting it was to take an oil can filled with gasoline, which was stored on a shelf over the machine, and squirt a teaspoonful of the liquid into each of the two petcocks. Then, by turning their two valves, you introduced the raw gasoline into the cylinders. Next, you pulled out the choke rod. Finally, you knelt in front of the heavy flywheel, almost in an attitude of prayer, took a good grip on its rim, and whirled it. It never caught on the first whirl. It often roared, if it consented to start at all that day, on the second whirl. But the memories of blistered hands and my sweat-soaked body during flat calms remind me that sometimes it would not start on the hundredth nor even the thousandth whirl. Once started, it was stopped by pressing a button which short-circuited the magneto, and the machine lapsed into blissful silence. Until acquiring *Tarheel* my education totally neglected marine engines, but I came to know that Kermath, each nick in its steel flywheel, each grease cup, each nut and bolt with an unforgettable intimacy. The operation of the engine, or at least its random failures to operate, led to some of our most memorable adventures.

Just forward of the engine was the galley sink and a large cast iron coal-burning Shipmate stove. Opposite it on the starboard side was an icebox with shelves over it for china and supplies. Forward of this neat little galley were settees on each side consisting of pipe berths with canvas laced to the frames and covered with thin mattresses. The backs of these settees were identical in construction, and by swinging them from their normal vertical position to a horizontal one, and attaching chains to ring bolts in the overhead, they transformed into upper berths. Just forward of the main cabin was the head, separated by a swinging door from the living spaces. At this point the full six-foot, one-inch head room ceased, and forward of the head, reachable only on hands and knees was space for sail storage, the anchor's chain locker, and spare gear.

That summer we learned how little we knew about cruising. In the first place, none of my all-male crew knew anything about cooking. Perhaps this was just as well, for the heat generated by our Shipmate coal stove on those hot summer days was so intense that the cabin became uninhabitable for hours after its use. As a result, cruising for us meant sailing from port to port, rowing ashore for all meals, and making every effort to avoid anchorages where restaurants were unavailable. The few times we were forced to cook our own meals, we cleaned the dishes by putting them in a net bag and dragging them behind the boat when we were underway. We had heard somewhere that the friction of the saltwater cleaned plates better than any human efforts, and the mere fact that the plates came up from their immersion in much the same condition as before did not discourage us.

We thoroughly explored the harbors on Long Island Sound within a thirty-mile radius of Rye, our home port, particularly favoring those which had restaurants near a landing dock. On our two-week vacation cruise, we ventured as far as Nantucket. As our experience with chartered *Tarheel* had been satisfactory, I bought her, and under my ownership she returned to Rye for a second summer.

No longer was *Tarheel* manned by an all-male crew. Jacquette, who had been born in Omaha and never been near the sea, volunteered to join up. Oddly enough, she, as the least-experienced member of the crew, taught us the most. After the very first day's sail, Jackie said, "I'm hungry. Let's cook something."

I said, "We have to go ashore to eat. We always do."

She asked, "Why? You have that great big stove. Doesn't it work?"

"Yes, it works," I told her, "but it takes quite a while to start it, and it gets everything so hot you can't stand it. Besides, we don't know how to cook."

Her eyes widened at this admission of masculine incompetence. "I've never heard such nonsense in my life. I'll teach you how to cook. There must be some kind of stove that's easy to start and doesn't get the cabin so hot." She descended to the cabin and conducted a survey of the pots, pans, plates, and silverware.

"Where is the cleaning stuff for the cooking utensils?" she asked.

I proudly explained our splendid method of dragging the dirty plates behind us in a mesh bag. Her nose wrinkled with distaste.

"Things are going to change if I'm going to sail with you," she said firmly, and they did.

The following week, I procured a two-burner alcohol stove which sat on the top of the Shipmate, and was held in place by two removable turnbuckles. Jackie brought aboard a large shopping bag full of dish towels, sponges, soap flakes, scouring pads, and the other paraphernalia for dish washing. Also a cookbook.

"All you have to do is read the directions," she assured us.

I must admit it was a tremendous improvement. The excellent meals she cooked and eventually taught us to cook gave birth to a personal adage: "The food on the boat is always better than the food on the beach."

Now we were able to explore lovely little bights with no restaurants and few houses to mar nature's beauty. It was a new and rewarding experience to seek out lovely anchorages rather than those bordering major towns. Lloyds Harbor, Mt. Sinai, Hamburg Cove, Cutty Hunk, Three Mile Harbor, and Point Judith replaced the busy anchorages of the year before. Cruising became fun even when the weather forced us to stay at anchor and read or play chess in our none too capacious cabin.

It was the intimacy of the cabin that caused me to

part with *Tarheel*. When Jackie and I were married, she said, "It's all very well when I was 'one of the boys' to have everyone know everything about everybody. But now that I am a respectable wife, instead of just the cook, I want a little privacy. Sleeping with three men in a 14-foot cabin, even though it only involves sleeping, is not my idea of the ultimate in pleasure. Let's get a bigger boat." So *Tarheel*, excellent teacher though she had proven to be, was replaced by the larger 38-foot *Rose*.

4

The Dinghy—
Eternal "Judas"

The small racing boats which instructed me in Marblehead were not suitable for port-to-port cruising, so I had no experience with that inevitable companion of all cruisers—the dinghy. However, on my first experience with a boat designed for cruising, I had a "cram" course in the floating menace that has trailed behind me down the years.

In the summer of 1935, when I had chartered *Tarheel* to receive my indoctrination in cruising, the boat's owner volunteered to pilot her with our help from her winter resting place in Atlantic Highlands, New Jersey, to my home port of Rye on Long Island Sound. The third Saturday of May that year, we embarked on my maiden voyage in *Tarheel* with the owner, Mr. Stewart, at the tiller.

Tidal currents around Marblehead are negligible and are not a factor to be taken into account in scheduling trips. But in New York harbor, it is virtually impossible for a small boat to progress if the current is unfavorable. Our early start was dictated by the fact that the tide would be flooding until about eleven that morning. Mr. Stewart made the engine procedure seem simple as we left our mooring under power. Once out in Sandy Hook Bay, we raised the sails, kept the engine running, and proceeded at maximum speed through the Narrows and up traffic-laden New York Harbor. It was exciting to sail past the skyscrapers without having the responsibility for pilotage or for avoiding collision with the plodding ferries or the busy tugs. Mr. Stewart was in command so all we had to do was keep a lookout for floating debris. With a strong current behind us, the Kermath at full speed, and a fresh gusty northwester filling our sails, we made fast progress up the East River to Hell Gate.

No reliable witness has described the gates to Hell. Dante and other poets who have portrayed the entrance were not familiar with the tide rip in the middle of New York's East River. Whether poets would consider Hell Gate an acceptable counterpart to the imaginary entrance of the nether regions, I do not know. My own belief is that whoever originally named this half-mile stretch of tumultuous water chose a fitting designation. On this May morning, Hell Gate was performing at its best. The maximum current of nearly six knots boiled the water into foam-crested whirlpools. The gusty wind, blowing against the current, added white-topped steep waves to the caldron. Man had played his part in the chaos as debris, wood crates, railroad ties, and all forms of driftwood whirled in the eddies of the narrow passage. It took *Tarheel* no more than five minutes to pass through the worst of it, and she suffered only wet decks from the slapping waves and the wind-swept spray. But the dinghy we were dragging behind us fared less well. Indeed, as we emerged from the tide rip and looked behind us, we saw that the 9-foot rowboat was swamped.

It was clear that towing this dead weight would not only slow our progress but also snap the rowboat's painter. It had to be bailed out without delay. The tidal current in the East River does not diminish much after Hell Gate, but as the stream widens the tide rips and whirlpools are less ferocious. There was no way to stop *Tarheel* and minister to the rowboat's needs; the current would have swept us along no matter in what direction we headed. So continuing on our way, we hauled the dinghy alongside and, armed with a bucket, I got in and bailed it out. Of course I was soaked, kneeling in the waterlogged rowboat, and the whole operation of sweeping along the narrow channel while I threw out buckets of polluted river water must have presented a ridiculous spectacle to those witnessing our progress from the shore. We had emerged from the river into Long Island Sound before I had completed my task and climbed back aboard *Tarheel*.

The name "Judas" suggested itself as a result of this episode, and every subsequent dinghy I have ever had has borne this shameful appellation. Obviously, the name changed the dinghy's gender designation from the graceful "she" used for all decent vessels, to an ignominious, treacherous "he." "Judas" has come in a variety of shapes, constructed of such diverse materials as wood, plywood, aluminum, and fiberglass. Only his behavior remains constant. "Judas" is dependable only in the sense that one can rely absolutely on his propensity for betrayal. The more horrendous the difficulty he can cause by his misbehavior, the more certain one can be that he will again earn his name. In calm weather, "Judas" follows quietly in the large boat's wake, his umbilical cord of rope showing no sign of strain. He merely awaits his opportunity. Let the wind pipe up, it matters not from which direction, "Judas" is ready to take advantage. In a favorable wind blowing from behind, "Judas" takes on a life of his own. His light weight permits him to come charging down the steep waves and butt his mother in the stern with his sharp nose. Or if he fails to hit her, he roars up abeam of her, then falls back with his painter slack, only to have it take up with a bang calculated to sever the rope. If the wind is from ahead, "Judas" hangs back, putting the maximum strain on his lead, thirstily gulping what spray he can fill himself with. His aim is to sink or at least become so full of water that he will act as a drag which must be bailed out before progress can be made.

If the mother boat is to be taken into a dock for water or fuel, "Judas" misses no opportunity to get in the way. As the engine is reversed to bring mother neatly alongside, "Judas" strives to wind his slack painter around the propellor. Or he shoots up, seeking to be crushed between the boat and the dock. In leaving a dock, he becomes entangled with pilings. He seeks every opportunity to hit moored boats as he is being towed, and he scores heavily when he can hit a piece of driftwood or become entangled with a fish weir or a lobster pot. He constantly strives, by shaking himself from side to side, to throw his oars overboard, and is particularly well satisfied if he can rid himself of just one of these tools, for it is virtually impossible to propel him with the remaining one.

Nor do his efforts cease when the boat is quietly anchored. Peacefully floating astern at the end of his painter as the crew turns in for a night's sleep, "Judas" can utilize errant currents of wind or, better still, tidal changes to slam into his mother in the middle of the night, thus arousing everyone to muzzle him. That is not all. He can arrange for a befogged crew of celebrants, returning late at night, to tie him up so ineptly that he can break his bond and drift to some hidden cove before his loss is discovered the next morning. He can capsize if an unwary or, more likely, an unsteady crew member gets into him one inch off his center line. There is only one way to disarm "Judas" completely. That is to bring him aboard his mother, turn him upside down, and lash him firmly so that he is unable to carry out any of his innumerable mischiefs.

One of the tenders most favored by cruising boats on the eastern seaboard is the Dyer dinghy. This 9-foot fiberglass rowboat was designed by my boyhood friend Raymond Hunt, who also helped design the excellent Boston Whaler outboard and the long-lived 110 and 210 Class of sailboats. The Dyer dinghy has one advantage; it is light—only weighing forty-five pounds. Therefore "Judas," in this form, is easy to bring aboard either by manhandling him or attaching him to the mainsail halyard and winching him aboard where he is helpless. His light weight is about his only attribute. He is tippy in the extreme. While he is easy to row, he takes spray over either bow or stern depending on the wind. He has styrofoam under his seats which prevents him from sinking like a stone, but he capsizes easily and is difficult to right again. He swamps in heavy rains or after being towed in hard winds, and I have found him easy to hate.

He also comes in a sailing model, which is fun to sail around harbors after the anchor is set. But this version is even more unsatisfactory as a tender than the simple rowboat. The spars for the single sail have to be carried on the mother boat's deck, but, for some reason, regardless of how tightly they are lashed down, on a hard thrash to windward, they are the first objects to go adrift. When towed, he is apt to leak through his centerboard trunk, and, no matter how much tape or rubber is used on the removable top to this trunk, the flood seems impossible to stem.

I have known experienced skippers to praise the fine qualities of their dinghies. I listen and marvel. But I remain unconvinced. To me "Judas," in no matter what form, could only deserve one alternative name— "Satan."

5

New Boats and the Perils of Commissioning

American advertising has encouraged the belief that nice new, shiny, bright machines work flawlessly. The idea is to get rid of that old decrepit car, refrigerator, or TV set and buy a brand-new, faultless replacement. The recall of hundreds of thousands of automobiles by Detroit manufacturers to correct dangerous mistakes in engineering or design has not discouraged this hopeful credo. Any new boat buyer who shares this simplistic faith in American know-how is in for a rude awakening.

While my first two boats, the O boat, *Rose,* and the Triangle, *Rose II,* were new from the builder's yard, I detected few flaws. The main reason for this apparent perfection was that I did not know enough about boats to discover a defect if it had been apparent to a blind man. Secondarily, these little sailboats were relatively simple examples of the boat builder's craft having neither motors, electricity, nor plumbing. *Tarheel,* with more complexities, had been sailed by an experienced yachtsman for years before I bought her, and whatever faults she had when new had long since been corrected.

The 38-foot cutter, *Rose,* our marital dream boat which offered Jackie the desired matronly privacy, was different in that she was virtually new. Built in 1936, she had been sailed for just two weeks when her owner was smitten by a heart attack. She had been hauled in Bristol, Rhode Island, soon after her owner had been taken to the hospital there. We took her over on a late May weekend in 1937, and, after the necessary provisioning, we started her impressive, virtually new engine and proceeded down Narragansett Bay.

We got nearly as far as Newport before a red warning light blinked on the instrument panel, indicating the engine was overheating. I peered over the stern to see if water was being expelled from the exhaust outlet. A thin trickle showed. The light had stopped blinking and was now a steady red danger signal. We turned off the motor, raised sail, and tacked to Point Judith's harbor of refuge. With the anchor down, we gathered for an inspection of the motor. It was big, and it was beautiful. Its fresh paint gleamed, its metal pipes shone brightly in the light. Twice the size and three times as powerful as *Tarheel's* little Kermath, it was awesome. It just did not work very well.

44

On the two-day trip to Rye, we fortunately had little use for the engine as the wind was fair. When we did use it, the red light came on after ten minutes of operation.

Despite the engine's irregular performance on the trip, we had some difficulty getting it to repeat its overheating routine for the mechanic that we persuaded to come aboard in our home harbor. After a while, however, the light blinked. The mechanic watched it till it glowed. Then he diagnosed.

"It's the Thermogard. I don't know why Gray has put these damn things on their perfectly good engine. Their idea is that when the sea water is cold, this temperature gauge closes down on the amount of sea water allowed to flow through the cooling system. When the sea warms up later in the summer, it allows more to be pumped through. I'll fix it or get a new one."

"What happens if we just take it off and throw it overboard?" I asked.

"Nothing. The engine will just run cooler in the spring which will give a little less power. But this engine is too big for this boat anyway."

We threw the Thermogard overboard. Murphy's law, which is well known to all yachtsmen, had operated as usual. (Note Murphy's Law: Anything that can go wrong, will, usually at the worst possible time.)

Like *Tarheel,* the 38-foot yawl *Skylark,* which I owned for twenty years had been sailed for several seasons by an experienced sailor, so whatever mistakes had attended her birth had long since been corrected. But *Shag,* my present 40-foot fiberglass yawl, offered a postgraduate education in what can go wrong with a new boat. We had not wanted to part with *Skylark,* but we planned to keep our boat in the Virgin Islands for a

Skylark, *a 39-foot auxiliary yawl, followed* Rose *as the author's fifth "teacher." Designed and built by Casey, with sails by Ratsey, she had a 4 cylinder Gray gasoline engine. She is shown here sailing on the St. John River in Canada. Kirstein owned Skylark from 1947 until 1967.*

number of years. It would have been murder of something we cherished to keep that aging wooden boat in the tropical Caribbean waters, whereas fiberglass is impervious both to the destructive marine growth and to the dry rot which are constant enemies in tropical waters.

Shag's name was suggested by the thousands of these birds (cormorants) that inhabit the Maine coast where we ordered the boat built.

Some creatures made a wrong choice of habitat at some early stage of their development. Whales, porpoises, sea lions, and seals probably should have chosen to live on land like the vast majority of other warmblooded mammals. In like manner, when they faced the choice between being fish or birds millions of years ago, cormorants should have chosen to remain fish. Their ability to swim either on the surface or underwater is equal to the fish that constitute their sole diet, but their ability to fly is minimal. Only with the greatest effort and the continuous flapping of their short wings are they able to propel themselves through the air. They cannot glide even for a few yards. No matter from what height they take off to start flight, for example from the top of a tall buoy, they rapidly sink to the water, beating their wings almost desperately and working their feet like paddles in the air. Only after they have touched the water do the birds begin to rise. This awkward takeoff has given birth to the bird watcher's adage, "A shag can't fly without getting his feet wet." Cormorants, which inhabit our coast from Maine to Florida and from Alaska to Mexico, are unafraid of man and with good reason. It is conceivable that starving men would eat a gull, indeed the survivors of a famous wreck on Boon Island reported that they did so. But the thought of eating a shag with the rank taste of his fish diet would turn the stomach of even a starving man. As a result of their fearlessness, these birds frequently decline to fly even when a vessel comes very near the rock, buoy, or piling on which they stand, often with their wings outstretched as if testing themselves for underwing odor. Upon being approached, the birds will turn their heads away so as not to view the approaching vessel in the same kind of falsely protective gesture as the ostrich which buries its head in the sand. It was because of our admiration as well as amusement at these rather ungainly birds that my wife and I agreed on *Shag* as the name for our boat.

Henry Hinckley Company of Southwest Harbor, Maine, has the reputation, and deservedly so, of being one of the top quality builders of fiberglass boats in the world. *Shag* was a sister to some fifty-eight identical hulls which had preceded her. So we were confident that whatever bugs had been found in the design or construction of these vessels had now been eliminated, and *Shag* would be flawless. Not only that, but Henry Hinckley himself, the presiding talent of this skilled yard, volunteered to supervise her commissioning. We ordered the boat in August and she was to be delivered on December 1 in Miami. Henry had a winter home in nearby Fort Lauderdale, and he was as good as his word about assisting us. He also assigned one of his own yard workmen to the task of preparing *Shag* for the ocean after her long truck ride from Maine. For a week, assorted workmen at the Bertram yard swarmed over the helpless vessel before she was launched. After launching, we took her up to Fort Lauderdale, where under Henry's guidance, more workmen labored for another week to put on finishing touches. If ever a new boat was well built (10,000 man-hours of labor had

Shag *a Bermuda 40, fibreglass yawl, is Kirstein's current
"teacher." Designed by Trippe and built by Hinckley, her
sails were made by Ratsey. Powered by a Westerbeke diesel
engine,* Shag *is shown racing in the Virgin Islands. Kirstein
has owned* Shag *since 1967.*

gone into her construction) and commissioned under expert supervision, *Shag* was it.

Rereading my log over the next three weeks reminds me of the following:

Item: Mainsail cover unuseable as no provision made for halyard winches. New mainsail cover ordered.

Item: Mizzensail looks like wet towel when sailing. Ordered it recut.

Item: Anchor chocks improperly installed. Sawed off one and one half inches of one side of anchor stock to make it fit.

Item: Tachometer does not work. Tightened connections.

Item: Light switches for navigation lights improperly labeled. Got electrician to correct reversed wiring.

Item: Alternator not charging batteries. Hammered voltage regulator, no solution. Tightened wires. Now works if electric icebox not used.

Item: Fathometer faulty. Replaced.

Item: Adapter used at dockside to change 110-volt shore current to 12 volts keeps blowing fuses. The temporary solution was to keep changing fuses.

Item: Neither electric nor hand bilge pumps work. Found scraps left by carpenters and mechanics had clogged pipes.

This is not a complete catalog by any means. None of these flaws were dangerous; all were annoying. They dispelled for all time any theory we may have tentatively held that new equals perfect.

The flaws that are discovered in new boats are irritating enough, but the ones that inevitably occur each spring, as the result of the ministrations of careless yard workmen, drive one to the point of madness. Every fall, I prepare a list of repairs that can only be effected when the boat is high and dry on land. These include replacement of worn-out parts, addition of new equipment, or work required below the water-line such as straightening propellor shafts or removing nicks in the propellor blades. Each year I review these repairs with the yard foreman of whatever yacht yard my boat is in, and he makes out the necessary job orders. I do not recall any occasion on which these specific repairs were not accomplished, but from their very accomplishment, new, and often more horren-dous, faults are introduced.

The most dangerous example of this annual disap-pointment resulted from one of the least complex repairs. One of the metal stanchions that supports the lifeline surrounding *Shag*'s entire deck became loose. All that was required was replacement of the lighter bolts with heavier ones. When we took delivery of the boat, I carefully checked this stanchion—firm as the Rock of Gibraltar. We set sail in a good wind soon after leaving the yard, and were perhaps fifteen miles out in the ocean when I glanced below. The cabin was half full of water to the point that the berths were submerged. I handed over the wheel and waded below. I heard an inrushing stream of water and followed the sound to an open hole through the hull where inflood-ing sea water was creating a miniature Niagara. I discovered that whatever workman had fixed the stanchion had removed a hose from the opening which discharged the bilge water when it was pumped. He not only failed to reconnect the hose, he hid it out of sight. I jammed rags into the opening to stem the flood and brought the boat around to the other tack so the hole would be above the water. It took two hours to bail the boat dry with buckets. I returned to the yard and tied up at the dock. Even though it had been some years since I had rehearsed the full range of profanity that I had learned during my three years in the Navy, that yard foreman was treated to the whole, juicy, rounded recitation.

Almost every yard foreman, up and down the coast, tells a story, which I always assumed was apocryphal, about a rival yard that launched a boat without shutting the sea cocks. A good raconteur is able to cause the listener to rock with laughter as he describes the scene of astonished workmen watching a boat slide smoothly down the ways and continue straight down to the bottom. It is not to be believed.

One spring the yard foreman of *Shag*'s winter resting place that year telephoned me at my home. "We are going to rewire your alternators," he told me. "But it won't cost you a cent."

"There was nothing wrong with the alternators," I assured him. "They charged the batteries just fine."

"Yes. Well they got wet."

"Got wet, for God's sake. How did that happen?"

"Well, when we launched the boat, the water came in as high as the alternators."

"Water came in?" I said. "You mean the boat sank."

"Yes," he shamefacedly admitted.

"Well, look, my friend, you rewire all the alternators you want if you need the practice. But on that boat you are going to put on brand, spanking new ones. Or else. Do you read me?"

"I read you loud and clear," he said.

So don't think it doesn't happen.

6

The Joys
and Hazards
of Women Aboard

While I owned *Tarheel,* I held firmly to the belief that
the ideal crew consisted of two or three able-bodied
men. On that rather unhandy little 30-footer with its
gaff rig, tiller steering, and hand-cranked engine, there
was logic to this theory. But when Jacquette and I
graduated to the larger 38-foot *Rose,* we discovered on
a honeymoon cruise that a man and wife alone can
easily handle modern boats up to forty feet in length.
A boat must have certain features for this kind of
cruising, and *Rose* had them. First the boat must steer
by wheel rather than by tiller. Women can steer
without tiring with a wheel which has gears to absorb
the rudder's pull. A tiller translates the rudder's forces
directly to the arm of the helmsman, and this pull,
strong at times when winds are high, taxes a woman's
strength. As long as the woman can steer under any

Rose, *the author's fourth "teacher," was an auxiliary cutter, 28' WL, 36' OA. Designed by Alden, she was built by Casey, had sails by Ratsey, and had a Gray 4 cylinder, 40 hp engine. She was Kirstein's instructor from 1938 to 1940.*

weather conditions, the man is perfectly capable of handling the sails, the anchor, and any other duties requiring greater strength. Second, the engine must have a self-starter, so that in case of emergency the woman at the wheel can start it instantly.

Rose's layout, similar to all her successors, was conventional, but the eight feet in length she boasted over *Tarheel* made her accommodations seem palatial. Beyond the galley, two bunks with a table between took up the main cabin. Then a head on one side and a large hanging locker for clothes separated the forward cabin which also had two full-length berths. Small boats do not offer the ultimate in privacy, but compared to our communal sleeping quarters on *Tarheel*, *Rose* seemed like the bridal suite in a large hotel. She had a beam of ten and a half feet and head room of six feet, one inch throughout all her living spaces. Jacquette and I worked out routines for all the usual situations of anchoring, retrieving a mooring, docking, putting up and reducing sail. On any maneuver where strength was required, for example, anchoring or retrieving the anchor, Jacquette steered and operated the engine. When steering required greater skill as in docking, I did it and Jacquette handled the lines.

Jacquette posed one problem that I have not encountered with many other women; she was fearless. I have sailed frequently with courageous people who overcame their fears, and I have sailed briefly with cowards. Jacquette had no fears to overcome even though she could not swim. Someone had thrown her in the water as a child on the theory that all animals can swim if they have to. This heroic treatment not only did not work, it made her adamant in refusing to try learning by more moderate methods. She refused to wear a life jacket or be hampered by a safety line.

The author at the wheel of his third Rose *in 1939.*

Her shortcoming did not inhibit her behavior on the boat in the least. She rowed the dinghy, moved quickly around the deck, and frequently urged that we sail when prudence dictated it would be wiser to remain at anchor.

Jacquette indoctrinated me in the lasting lesson that hair, at least clean hair, is all-important. Most of the time while cruising, our day's destination was a matter of indifference to Jackie. She understood that changing wind conditions, adverse tidal schedules, and other factors could cause me to change my mind half a dozen times during the day as to where we would anchor for the night. However, by the fifth day after the last shampoo, she would ask, "Where are we going to be tonight?"

"Come on, Jackie. You tell me what direction the wind will be and how strong, and I'll tell you precisely where we'll be."

"Well, that's all very fine, but I want to go ashore in a town big enough to have a hairdresser."

I might be able to stall off the inevitable by one day, but if more than six days went by without this cleansing rite, sullenness would be replaced by mutiny. The ultimatum usually was, "I get my hair done today, or you get yourself another girl."

Every woman I have subsequently sailed with played minor variations on the same theme. After a week, hair takes precedence over such minor considerations as weather, convenience, or future commitments.

Jacquette was an ideal crew, but historical events dictated that I take an all-male cruise on a far larger vessel, painted the Navy's gray, with her guns always manned and ammunition in the ready boxes. When I returned, I found Jackie had resigned as mate.

After the war, I discovered from personal experi-

Jacquette in the cockpit of Tarheel, *1938.*

ence why so many men "swallow the anchor" after they are married. Elinor loved day sailing; at least she said she did. However, after we married and tried extended cruising, problems developed. Elinor had red hair and a very light complexion. Prolonged exposure to sun and wind wrought havoc with her natural endowment of beauty. In addition, she did not like the "tilting." No matter how frequently I explained that boats are designed to heel over while going to windward and that there is no chance of capsizing, her fears remained unabated. Curiously, in many conversations with men whose wives decline to sail, I have found this dislike of tilting heads the list of reasons that are given. Whether Freud would have some explanation for this incurable fear, I do not know. I do know it is commonplace. As sailing is for fun, there is no point in having a miserable mate aboard. For the most part Elinor stayed ashore, and I resumed all-male cruising.

On the night of July 26, 1956, *Skylark* was anchored in Nantucket Harbor. Except for the way that the events of that night affected my subsequent life, there was nothing particularly memorable about it. The moon shone down on the placid harbor through wisps of fog, and *Skylark* rode easily at her anchor. The next morning as I tuned the radio for the official weather report, I learned that the impossible had happened. Two huge ocean liners, the *Andrea Doria* and the *Stockholm* had collided some forty miles south of where we lay at anchor, and the *Andrea Doria* had sunk. Modern ocean liners cannot sink; at least they are not supposed to be that vulnerable. Yet the radio was chronicling one of the most dramatic rescue operations in the long history of the sea. The *Ile de*

France, outward bound from New York to Cherbourg, had picked up the SOS. At first her captain declined to believe the emergency signal; but, when it was confirmed, he reversed course, coaxed the last ounce of power out of her mammoth engines, and with eyes glued to the radar scope sped back to the rescue. She coasted to a stop near the sinking hulk, every light ablaze, her lifeboats manned and swung out on their davits. A Tidewater oiler, bound from Boston to the Gulf ports, picked up the SOS and came pounding through the fog banks at her best speed to add her two lifeboats to the rescue operation. And, of course, the Coast Guard dispatched to the scene nearly everything in the vicinity that could float.

In the city room of the *New York Times,* a hastily summoned army of editors and rewrite men waited impatiently for the eyewitness account of the disaster from one of their crack foreign correspondents who was traveling on the ship with his wife and child. But Camille Cianfarra never sent the dispatch. He lay dead with his crushed child near him in the bowels of the *Andrea Doria* where the Swedish vessel's bow had found him. His badly injured wife lay pinned in the wreckage for hours until the heroic efforts of a room steward, working alone, freed her and accomplished her transfer to a rescue vessel.

I met Jane Cianfarra early the following summer. She had recently ended a long hospital stay and had resumed her work on the *New York Times* as a fashion reporter. She was the saddest person I have ever met. The loss of her husband and child, her own broken body, and the recurring nightmares of the collision kept tears near the surface. I invited her for a day of sailing on *Skylark* with the couple who had introduced us. It was the first time she had been near the sea since

Jane taking the Newfoundland, "Skipper," for a ride on Skylark, *1961.*

the disaster, and the beauty of the day, the soft breeze, and the spectacle of the racing fleet displaying multi-colored spinnakers brought an occasional fleeting smile to her habitually tragic features.

In late September we were married and embarked on *Skylark* for a two-week honeymoon. Jane was apprehensive. The sea had demanded a dreadful toll of her, and her fears were deeply ingrained. But nature paid her back in small measure for her loss. For two weeks, the New England fall was at its glorious best: the yellow harvest moon on crisp nights, the sun shining with Indian summer warmth, the wind steady but soft from the northwest, the sea smooth, and for two weeks not a drop of rain. The foliage was a blazing mixture of red and gold as we sailed up the Connecticut River to the outskirts of Hartford. Exhausted by the fresh air, the swimming in the still warm sea, and the unaccustomed exercise of sailing, Jane slept soundly without medication for the first time in over a year. She was hooked on sailing. As we picked up our mooring in Mamaroneck after a perfect cruise, I warned her, "It's not always like that. Sometimes it's uncomfortable and damp, sometimes it blows, some-times there's fog. But if you know what you are doing, there is no more danger than there is in driving to the grocery store."

"You don't have to worry about me," Jane assured. "Except for fog, I'd love every minute of it." And for ten years she did.

Jane, like other women, asked about the tilting. I went to a local toy store and bought an inexpensive kewpie doll which rocked on a rounded lead base. "Let's see you capsize it," I challenged her. No matter how it was pushed, the doll always returned to an upright position.

The author at anchor off Jonesport, Maine, in Skylark, *1952.*

"A boat is the same thing," I assured her. "The keel has the same effect as the lead base of the doll. You can tilt it, but only so far. After that a sail will tear or something will break, but the boat can't tilt any further." Jane, who was the most courageous human being I ever knew for she had more justifiable fears than other people, accepted the explanation so the "tilting" no longer bothered her.

The following summer, we cruised for a few weeks in Chesapeake Bay. Despite frequent groundings, Jane gained confidence in *Skylark* and her skipper. We took short cruises along Long Island Sound as far as Block Island, Sag Harbor, and Shelter Island. I carefully avoided running in fog, and by the end of summer, Jane wanted to spend even more time sailing. That winter, we chartered a boat in the Virgin Islands and fell in love with the area. Here the idea of *Shag* was conceived. Like a human baby, she took nine months to develop from conception to reality.

We discussed bringing *Skylark* down to the islands, but I had to tell Jane that the aging wooden boat would not be able to survive the inevitable dry rot spawned by blazing sun and frequent drenching showers. Neither of us wanted a glass boat. At first we tried to get a naval architect to design a wooden boat with a protective fiberglass shield over the hull. We discovered that because glass and wood have different expansion characteristics in changing temperatures, the idea was not practical. We went to some factories where glass boats were being produced and hated what we saw.

The following summer we cruised on the Maine coast. Jane loved the coves, the spruce trees coming down nearly to the water's edge, the seals sunning themselves on the tide bared rocks, and the hills of Mt. Desert Island which reminded her of her native northwest. She hated the fog. I took every possible precaution not to be caught in it. When the nearly inevitable gray clouds caught us, Jane's hands trembled, but only once did she retreat in hysterical tears to the privacy of the cabin.

When we reached Southwest Harbor, we took *Skylark* to Henry Hinckley's yard for minor engine repairs. We got into a long conversation with Mr. Hinckley, and Jane outlined our problem of wanting an easily maintained glass boat while at the same time, for aesthetic reasons, we despised the synthetic material. Henry invited us aboard his own Bermuda 40, *Jaan.* The cabin was completely panelled in mahogany, the cabin sole was a striped inlay of holly on teak. No glass was visible from any part of the living compartment. Henry discussed the excellent sailing qualities of the Tripp-designed boat with me, but I was already familiar with their splendid racing record and their reputation for sturdiness under adverse conditions. The compact diesel engine was an added incentive; I was frequently alarmed by the smell of gasoline fumes that were never entirely absent from *Skylark.*

"I don't like the cabin layout," Jane said as she inspected *Jaan.* "I want only two berths in the main cabin. I want a fireplace, and I don't like the pot and pan storage arrangement."

"That is the way we make them," Henry said firmly.

"That's too bad," Jane replied with equal determination. "I guess we're just going to have to look further."

"I'll tell you what I'll do," the boat builder conceded. "If you order the boat now in August when my work force is relatively idle, I'll make you any kind of a main cabin layout that my head carpenter says is possible. But if you delay, I just can't fit custom cabinetmaking into my production schedule."

"When would we get it if we ordered it now?" I asked.

"In December," he answered, "and I'll deliver it to Miami and help with the commissioning."

In due course, the head carpenter came aboard *Skylark,* and we showed him exactly the features we wanted in the main cabin of the new boat.

"I'll work on it," he promised. "You're cruising. Come back in a few days, and I'll see what I can work out."

A few days later, the head carpenter showed us just what could be done and what could not. Fortunately, nearly everything Jane wanted was possible. The berths, unencumbered by accompanying transoms, could slide out to a luxurious thirty-inch width, and they could accommodate six-inch foam rubber mattresses. The storage space gained by eliminating two berths was ample for months of cruising. Jane was enthusiastic so I walked up to Mr. Hinckley's office to confirm our decision and make financial arrangements. To my surprise, I saw my name next to a hull number already posted on the production board. The builder had correctly guessed our decision even before we made it.

Planning the household gear that was to go aboard *Shag* gave Jane the idea for a book. She told me, "Moving into the cabin of a boat to live is like furnishing a doll's house. For example, the broom should be a child's broom, not the big thing we keep tripping over on *Skylark.*"

I suggested that with her reportorial experience, her mounting love of sailing, and her forthcoming experience at commissioning a brand new boat, she might have material for an article for a woman's magazine. A few weeks later, as her equipment lists grew and her

Shag *being commissioned at Bertram's Miami Yard in December, 1966.*

voluminous notes gathered on different kinds of blankets, fitted sheets, and vari-colored towels differing for each crew member, she announced that there might indeed be enough material for a book.

Jane refused adamantly to cruise with other women on the boat. She said, "They want to help and all they do is get in the way." I told her it was difficult to tell our married friends that only the husband was invited. "We have no trouble sailing the boat ourselves," she said. "I get along fine with women ashore, but we're not going to have them on this boat." And we didn't. This rule reduced the size of our crew, but it also reduced the friction to the vanishing point.

The summer after *Shag*'s delivery, Jane and I brought her up the Inland Waterway from Miami to our home port, Mamaroneck. In mid-June, I invited my sister, some thirteen years older than I am, to inspect it. In all the years I had sailed boats, she had never been aboard one or shown the slightest interest, so I was somewhat surprised when she readily accepted my invitation. I proudly demonstrated all of *Shag*'s splendid features to her. I displayed the stove which was hung in gimbals so cooking could be accomplished even in rough seas. I showed her the comfortable berths that pulled out to the size of a single bed on land. I pointed out all of the commodious storage facilities, the shower which had been a godsend on many occasions, the relatively large boat's library and adequate chart stowage. When the tour was completed I asked, "What do you think?"

Unhesitatingly she replied, "I'll tell you what I think. I think Jane is the most remarkable woman I ever met in all my life."

7

Rivers, Canals, and Bridges

I had virtually no experience with piloting a boat on the confined waters of a river when in the spring of 1936 I went to Passaic, New Jersey, to bring *Tarheel* from that inland harbor to Rye on Long Island Sound. In *Rose,* I had once been towed through the narrow, winding Annisquam Canal and twice through the longer Cape Cod Canal. I had been aboard *Tarheel* but not in command the previous summer on her passage up New York's East River. However, nothing in our backgrounds prepared Jacquette, my friend Earl, and myself for the adventures that awaited us that last Sunday in May.

We hadn't studied the charts of the route between Passaic and Rye which we had with us, but we were confident that our successful transit of the East River the year before would preclude our having trouble. However, our self-assurance wavered as we concentrated on the chart prior to leaving the dock. Not only is the Passaic River a narrow and tortuous waterway, but it is crossed by some twenty bridges before it even enters New York's lower bay, and, in order to permit our mast to pass under, sixteen of these had to be opened. Some of the drawbridges accommodated automobile traffic, but by far the largest number were railroad bridges which accommodated mainlines of the Pennsylvania, Erie-Lackawanna, and the Chesapeake and Ohio. We knew nothing of drawbridges, never having passed under one, but we knew enough about railroads to foresee that if trains were scheduled, bridges were not going to be very prompt in opening to let us through. The tide tables predicted that the current would flood in our favor in Hell Gate around noon, so about ten in the morning, we cast off our dock lines, and, with the ebbing current adding its momentum to Kermath's efforts, we started down the Passaic River. Earl had had the foresight to inquire from me what the procedure was for attracting the attention of bridge tenders, and I had discovered in that indispensable volume *Coast Pilot* that the proper procedure was to blow three blasts on a fog horn. Our horn was merely a galvanized tube which made a noise much like a New Year's Eve party favor when you blew through it. As we approached the first of the sixteen bridges, Earl blew the required three times. Nothing happened. Absolutely nothing. By moving the clutch handle, I shifted the motor into neutral, and, while this eliminated the speed that Kermath gave us, it did not stop the forward motion aided by the tidal current. We were drifting down on the closed bridge, and I had a vision of the mast crashing down around our heads.

"Put it in reverse," Earl yelled.

I threw the clutch handle into the reverse position. Two things happened almost simultaneously. First, as our speed was stemmed by the reverse thrust of the propellor, "Judas," with the aid of the current, came alongside, making every effort to entwine his painter in the thrashing propeller. Secondly, it was apparent that the engine in reverse did not have enough power to offset the speed of the ebbing tide. Just before our bow got irretrievably intertwined with the bridge, I pushed the clutch bar forward and swung the boat 180 degrees back toward Passaic.

"This is kind of fun," Jackie said. "We'll be able to see a lot more of beautiful, historic old Passaic."

"God Almighty," I replied, "we damn near took the mast right out of her. See Passaic, indeed. Earl, give that guy three more blasts on the horn."

Again nothing happened. We proceeded slowly upstream about a hundred yards when a long freight train began roaring over the bridge.

"Oh," Earl said, "no wonder it didn't open."

After the train had passed, lights began flashing on the bridge, and three blasts on a horn came from the operator's tower.

"It's going to open now," Jackie announced. "That red light has turned green."

"What red light?" I asked.

"The one in the middle of the span."

Neither Earl nor I had noticed it in our concentrated attention on whether the bridge would lift.

"Listen, Jackie," I said, "Don't hesitate to call our

attention to these fascinating details if *we* don't see them. Otherwise we're all going to be killed."

We headed back for the bridge, and by the time we got there it had lifted enough to let us through.

"Only fifteen more to go," I said cheerfully, but my hand was trembling as I held the tiller.

As we proceeded down the stream, some bridges opened even before we tooted the three blasts, but most of them delayed their opening until at least one train had passed over. We used the same circling technique successfully no matter how long the delay. By the time we had passed under the third or fourth, we felt like veterans; at least we no longer endangered the vessel each time we came to one of these movable barriers across our path.

I encountered plenty more bridges on my cruises in *Rose* and *Skylark,* but they were all the high ones that span the Connecticut River or the Cape Cod Canal, and both of these bodies are wide enough to maneuver if the single railroad bridge that spans each one is in a down position. It was not till the first time I took *Skylark* up Canada's beautiful St. John River that another noteworthy encounter with a bridge occurred. Off the wide, winding one hundred-mile-long river is a beautiful thirty-mile freshwater lake. Grand Lake is connected to the St. John River by a tiny, narrow, twisting stream, the Jemseg River. I have traversed the Jemseg many times since I first saw it in 1954, and I still am somewhat apprehensive about this little channel that is barely wide enough to turn a 40-foot boat around. That first time, *Skylark* was throttled down to a dead slow pace. We saw on the chart that there was a low bridge, which would have to open, at the little village of Jemseg before we could explore the beauties of the lake. As we approached the bridge, we blew the customary three blasts. Nothing happened. There was no bridge tender, nor could we see a human being closer than a half a mile away. We blew again. Still nothing.

"Let's anchor," I said, and we did right in the middle of the narrow stream. About a half an hour passed; we blew three more times. A man leading a horse ambled down the hill from the village. When the pair got to the bridge, he yelled to us.

"I heard you. But I wanted to finish plowing the row I had begun." In a leisurely way, he hitched the horse to a turntable and then drove the animal in a circle. The bridge creaked slowly open. We started the motor, raised the anchor, and proceeded. We waved as we went through and shouted our thanks. In those days, I don't think the traffic on the Jemseg interrupted his agricultural pursuits very often. Today, a bridge, high enough to accommodate a standard-size mast, crosses this tiny stream, but the ghost of the horse and the turntable persists, at least in my memory, whenever I return to this bucolic scene.

I received my graduate degree in passing under bridges in my three passages up the Intracoastal Waterway from Florida to New York in *Shag*. I have not counted recently, but my recollection is that there are one hundred thirty one of these barriers to progress between Miami and New York City. They come in all sizes and shapes. Some lift, some swing, and some rise from one side. As the traffic on the waterway is heavy, bridge tenders are alert, and, most of the time, it is unnecessary to blow the horn as the bridge is already opening by the time the vessel is ready to pass under.

The enemy on the confined stretches of the waterway is not the bridges, but the hundreds of powerboats

The Skipper trying to get a passing powerboat to slow down on Intercoastal Waterway in 1971.

that throw off huge wakes in their path. I noticed that the boats passing in the opposite direction were thoughtful and considerate in slowing their engines to a crawl so that their wakes were reduced to ripples. However, for some reason I was unable to understand, the boats going in the same direction threw up wakes which rocked us so violently that anything not securely fastened was thrown to the deck, spilled, or broken. Once again, I was fated to learn the hard way the explanation for the thoughtless powerboat skippers.

On a particularly narrow stretch of the waterway, a 50-foot powerboat overtook us. We were in the middle of lunch. Bowls of soup, glasses of milk, and sandwiches were precariously balanced next to us. The powerboat, forced to pass near us by the confines of the channel, threw up a horrendous wake. Everything spilled. I was furious. I shook my fist at the powerboat's skipper, but he appeared not to notice, obviously indifferent to the discomfort he had caused.

Around five in the afternoon, we docked *Shag* at one of the hundreds of marinas that border the waterway. Just ahead of us, tied up to the same dock, was the offending 50-footer. My impulse was to walk over and give that skipper a piece of my mind, but, on second look, I saw that the helmsman was a professional captain, suitably garbed in his khaki uniform and with the physique of a professional wrestler. I decided silent contempt would be a more prudent stance.

Despite my pantomimed attitude, the captain strolled down the dock and stood beside *Shag*.

"Pretty sore when I passed you, weren't you?"

"I sure as hell was," I replied.

"It was your fault," he told me blandly.

"My fault?" I said angrily, for the moment forgetting prudence.

"Let me see if I can explain something to you," he said. "How fast does your boat go?"

"Six knots," I told him.

"O.K. So if I want to pass you, I have to go eight knots. At that speed, my boat throws up its maximum wake. At fifteen knots it throws up less, but you can't go that fast on the waterway. If you had thrown your engine in neutral and drifted to a stop, I would have passed you at two knots, and there would have been no wake whatever."

"I never thought of that," I admitted.

"Most people on sailboats don't," he told me. "Just come to a stop when someone is overtaking, and you won't have any trouble."

It was an uncomfortable, but memorable, method of learning that overtaking powerboats are just as considerate as passing ones, if one has enough wit to make it easy for them.

The most frightening experience I ever had in confined waters, even worse than my Passaic River introduction to bridges, occurred after I was thoroughly experienced in this type of pilotage. It cured me, once and for all, of a miserly habit I had developed of saving charts and using them again and again until they practically fell apart. Some people save twine, others old magazines. I saved charts. My theory was that the contours of the ocean bottom do not change in centuries, so why buy new charts every year?

It was a beautiful August day in 1964 when we left Jonesport, Maine, with our day's destination Campobello Island. A cold front had come in during the night, and a whistling northwest wind had dissipated the fog, leaving the coast of Maine a sparkling panorama. We set *Skylark*'s big spinnaker, and, with the strong flood tide assisting us up the Grand Manan Channel, we raced for the Lubec Narrows which forms the boundary between Canada and the United States. We took in all sail and started the engine as we rounded West Quoddy head with its easternmost American lighthouse. The narrow channel that separates the mainland from the Canadian island of Campobello twists and turns as well a having a ferocious tide as billions of gallons of water rush through the narrow entrance to enter Passaquamody Bay. I followed our passage past the channel buoys on my ancient chart, but I had been there so often before that I felt I barely needed any aid to navigation.

One of my crew said, "I didn't know they had a bridge across here."

"They don't," I said confidently. "There's a ferry between Lubec and the island."

"Take a look," he said.

There, a half a mile ahead was a bridge, new since my last visit and, of course, not shown on my out-of-date chart.

"I wonder how high it is," I said, as I looked up at *Skylark*'s mast towering fifty feet above the boat.

"Well, I guess we're going to find out," he said. "There is no way in the world that we can turn around and buck this current."

I throttled the engine down to dead slow, but the current swept us inexorably toward the bridge.

"Everyone get in the bow," I ordered. "If we hit, the mast will fall backwards."

Alone in the cockpit, I kept my eye on the bridge. "Perhaps we'll make it," I thought.

At the moment we passed beneath the highest part of the span, the yacht club burgee at the top of the mast snapped back, but we had made it with perhaps a foot to spare. If fate had ordained the delay of our passage by an hour when the huge tide would have been a foot higher, we would have struck.

As we docked at the customs dock on Campobello to complete formalities for entering Canada, I asked the inspector, "When did they put up that bridge?"

"Oh, it's just been finished," he said proudly.

"How high is it?" I asked.

"It's supposed to give a clearance of forty eight feet at high tide. Of course, it's higher when the tide is low."

"The chart doesn't show it at all," I told him.

"Oh, the new ones do," he assured me.

My chart-hoarding days ended abruptly at that moment.

8

Passages Offshore

Unlike daytime port-to-port cruising, voyages which consume at least twenty-four hours and take the vessel out of sight of land are the adventures of sailing. Because such passages require that each crew member sleeps part of the time, watches must be set and food prepared despite the gyrations of the boat. Finally, as familiar landmarks are beyond view, the nagging question eventually arises as to whether the harbor you are aiming for is the one you will reach.

The curving arc of the New England coast from Cape Cod to Portland invites the yachtsman with a limited schedule to sail a direct course for Maine, rather than follow the indentation of the coast in port-to-port cruising. The distance from the Cape Cod Canal or Provincetown to Monhegan Island at the foot of Penobscot Bay is about a hundred miles, a distance that can easily be traversed in twenty-four hours, whereas following the curvature of the coast to the same point is about twice the distance, and consumes some five days of daytime port-to-port runs.

Of the many passages across the Gulf of Maine that I've made in different boats a few stand out in my memory because of some curious event that occurred, the difficulty in making a landfall, or just a whopping navigational error that ended us up where we did not plan to be. There was, for example, the night we entered Heaven. On the second night out of Marblehead bound for St. John, New Brunswick, *Skylark* was ghosting along in a very light breeze. It had been a slow passage with the prevailing southwest wind gentle enough to give us steerage way thus discouraging use of the motor, but barely enough to drive us at more than three or four knots. At three o'clock in the morning, we were at least twenty-five miles off the coast of Maine, drifting along, when I first heard the faint strains of "Abide with Me." The notes of the hymn being played on the organ were so faint that I thought at first I must have fallen asleep and been dreaming. I left the wheel, stamped my feet to make sure I was fully awake, and again listened. There it was again, faint but distinct. There were no words, just the clear notes of the organ, but I had sung the words so many times in school chapel, that I had no difficulty in imagining the voices of the heavenly choir which was performing. If I were to enter the Pearly Gates into immortality, I had no intention of doing so alone. I called my shipmates. Sleepy heads poked up the companionway.

"What's up?" one asked, obviously indignant at being called on a night so placid that there was barely a ripple on the water.

"Hear anything?" I asked.

After a moment's silent listening, one said, "Yes, I hear a hymn. We must be passing a church on the shore."

"A church on the shore?" I said. "At three o'clock in the morning? Anyway we are at least twenty miles from shore and it isn't Sunday."

By now we were all wide awake. We may have been lulled by the absence of all normal hazards of the sea, but the direct intervention of the Divine Presence was unnerving. Silence. Then very softly the strains of "Onward Christian Soldiers" reached us out of the stillness.

"What the hell is going on?" one of my shipmates asked in a tone calculated to rout whatever angels might be performing.

No one answered. For the next hour, the heavenly instrumentalist played a repertoire of hymns, all on an organ, which became fainter and fainter as the first light of dawn reached us. We scanned the sea. Nothing was in sight. Clearly, we had all witnessed a miracle.

Around noon, we drew abreast of Cutler, Maine, as we closed the land. The wind was still light and the strong Fundy tide was about to set against us down the Grand Manan Channel. We decided to enter Cutler, get a lobster dinner and rest before proceeding on to St. John. Tied up at the fish pier, we saw a large white powerboat with a huge blue cross painted on its side. Two of us rowed ashore after anchoring, and approached this sturdy craft with the name *Sunbeam* painted on its transom.

"Hi," I said to the man on deck, "Were you playing hymns last night on an amplifier?"

He laughed. "Oh, did you hear us?" he asked. "We play music to keep us awake on a night run. *Sunbeam* is the mission boat that visits the islands. We perform weddings and render other religious services to the people who can't get ashore."

"We thought you were angels," I told him.

"We hope a few of the islanders would agree," he smiled.

Then there was the night at Annisquam. The run across the Gulf of Maine from Boothbay to Gloucester is not long—perhaps eighty miles or so—and with luck it can be completed during daylight hours in the summer months. But this time luck was against us. We started at first light in a flat calm and made good progress with the motor for the first few hours. The Maine coast had barely dropped out of sight astern when the prevailing southwest wind came in with sufficient force so that the motor no longer was useful. We had a long, long tack down the coast out of sight of land in the typical haze that accompanies these winds. At sunset the wind died and the motor was called on for another stint. At one o'clock in the morning we had passed the Isles of Shoals and sighted the powerful light on Thacher Island. We were tired, so I decided to anchor off Annisquam on the north side of Cape Ann rather than go all the way around into Gloucester Harbor. There is a long sandbar that jets out from Annisquam, so this narrow channel cannot be entered safely at night. But it was calm, so we looked forward to anchoring in Ipswich Bay, getting a few hours sleep and in the morning entering the canal from Annisquam to Gloucester, which cuts off the long trip around the cape. We altered our course and, shortly, sighted the flashing light at Annisquam. By three we were anchored a safe distance from the bar and prepared to go below for a final cup of coffee and sleep. It was not to be.

A large fishing trawler, perhaps eighty feet long, typical of the vessels based in Gloucester began to circle us at slow speed. I had had every confidence in the safety of our anchorage having taken cross bearings on both the nearby Annisquam lighthouse and the more distant ones at Ipswich and Newburyport. But what was the trawler doing? Was he trying to tell us something by his circling maneuvers? Trawler captains are amoung the most experienced seamen in the world. This vessel would not be circling us and shining his powerful searchlight at us unless something was wrong. After twenty minutes, the large vessel approached to within twenty yards. A voice across the water yelled,

"Hey, Captain, do you know where the hell you're at?"

My confidence by now was thoroughly shaken. I glanced once more at the three lights on the shore and yelled back, "Well, I think I do."

The trawler's voice came back, "All right, where are you?"

I told him I thought I was in Ipswich Bay, with the Annisquam light close aboard, and the Ipswich and Newburyport lights visible to the northwest.

A long silence, presumably while the trawler captain checked the accuracy of my answer in much the way a college professor might have to refer to a book before correcting an erring student.

The voice again, "Hey, Captain, are you going to enter the canal in the morning?"

I yelled back an affirmative answer.

"Wake us up when you leave. We want to follow you in."

The trawler withdrew to a safe distance, and we heard her anchor chain rattle out.

"Now I have seen absolutely everything," I told my

shipmates. "A fishing captain asking a yachtsman where he is and then wanting to be piloted into his own home port."

Around sunrise, we raised our anchor and I circled the trawler. She seemed huge compared to *Skylark*, and her newly painted green sides reflected the sunlight. I yelled as we neared the vessel. "Hey, we are going in now."

A sleepy head poked out of the pilothouse. "Wait a few minutes while we get the anchor up."

"What's wrong?" I asked.

"Oh, we're just a couple of carpenters from the builder's yard in Rockland trying to deliver this boat to the owners. We don't go to sea much, and we got kind of confused."

My short-lived feeling of superiority evaporated. Here, two craftsmen without experience had brought this huge vessel, usually requiring a crew of five or six men all the way from Penobscot Bay, and while shaken by uncertainty had nevertheless ended up precisely where they intended.

I waved, circled the trawler twice while they raised their anchor, and then led the way down the buoyed channel to the canal entrance.

A few summers later, we made much the same run, but the surprise in store on this one was not furnished by an errant trawler. Again we left Boothbay bound this time for Marblehead. My crew was Milton, a shipmate from Navy days, now a bank officer, who had spent many vacations over the postwar years sailing with me on *Skylark*. He was both experienced and competent so we expected no navigational problems, particularly in view of the magnificent weather. After several days of fog, a thunderstorm had passed during the night, and a sparkling sunny day with a fine northwest wind furnished unlimited visibility. It was so clear that, even as we took our departure from Sequin Island, I did not rig the patent log which records the miles run because I was confident that we could recognize points on the distant coast all the way along.

It was a beautiful sail with the spinnaker set. Every few hours one of us would relieve the other at the wheel. A shark swam lazily around the boat and we first threw orange rinds at him, then got out the boat's .22 calibre rifle and shot at him. We missed. We paid no attention to pilotage, nor did we bother plotting positions. We could see to infinity. The sunset was a glorious red and gold that presaged a crystal night and good weather on the morrow. Every star in the heavens appeared in due course; it was magnificent. We expected to reach Cape Ann around midnight, and we kept a desultory lookout for the lights that warned mariners of its presence. We did not see the lighthouses, but around midnight the navigation lights of a number of vessels crossed our bow on a course at right angles to our own.

"Where do you suppose those boats are bound?" Milt asked.

"Well, the only harbor in there is Gloucester," I told him.

"Maybe that's where they are all going," he suggested.

"We're not even at Cape Ann yet," I told him. "Besides sometimes those fishing boats don't know what the hell they're doing," and I recounted my adventure with the lost trawler.

We sailed happily along over the smooth sea on this beautiful night. By three o'clock in the morning, we were both aware that we were lost and really had no idea where we were. I changed course to close with the land. At four o'clock, I sighted a red flashing light on our bow.

"I'll go below and look up that red flasher," I told Milt, and I proceeded to study the chart. I searched the whole coastline from the Isles of Shoals to Marblehead on the chart. No red flasher.

"Milt," I said, "you won't believe this, but there isn't a red flasher on the whole damn coast of New England."

He laughed. "Maybe not," he replied, "but we're about to come abreast of one."

I returned to the chart. Milt called down from the wheel. "Hey, there is a lobster boat. Let's ask him where we are."

"Ask him?" I was outraged by the suggestion. "In absolutely clear weather ask someone where we are? I'd rather shoot myself."

We circled the red flasher until the first light of dawn disclosed the familiar outlines of Scituate Harbor. Scituate is some twenty-five miles south of Cape Ann. We had passed the cape at midnight without recognizing it. The lights we saw on the passing vessels were on trawlers bound for Gloucester, but this time they knew what they were doing.

"Well, it was a beautiful sail," I told Milt as we entered the harbor.

"That was a real triumph of navigation," Milt said, rocking with laughter. While this happened years ago I cannot expect even now to sail with Milt without at some point hearing that word of ignominious memories—"Scituate."

One other passage across the Gulf of Maine ended up with a missed landfall, but this time it was not due to negligence or inattention to navigation. We left Vinelhaven at the foot of Penobscot Bay on a fair summer day bound for Provincetown. My crew on this occasion consisted of three men, all experienced. Martin, the doctor, who volunteered as medical officer and navigator. Milt agreed to be morale officer, but his only contribution to this duty was from time to time to repeat the unwelcome word "Scituate" and then break into peals of laughter. Carl had been an infantry officer in World War II and had stepped on a land mine in the Battle of the Bulge. After a year or more in a veterans' hospital, the government had furnished him with an aluminum leg which worked very well, but obviously restricted his movements to the cabin and cockpit. To offset this inability to assist in sail handling, he took more than his fair share of steering duties.

The passage was entirely uneventful. Smooth sea and a fair wind furnished *Skylark* with the conditions that she liked the best. Every few hours, Martin would read the dial on the patent log, go below and put a tiny cross on the chart on the direct line to Provincetown. Conditions remained the same during the night. For once the west wind did not die at sunset, but continued gently through the night. It was the kind of a summer sail one dreams about during a February blizzard. Occasionally the two who were on watch would see the lights of another vessel, but for the most part only the stars, the phosphorescent wake, and the gurgle of the bow wave marked this placid night.

Soon after dawn, I said to Martin, "We ought to be able to see Cape Cod by now. Where do you figure we are?"

"We're within twenty miles of it," he assured me. "We'll see the Pilgrims' Monument any time now."

But we didn't. By ten o'clock, the log showed we

had run more than our distance. Still no Provincetown. We took turns staring ahead through the binoculars. No land.

"This is crazy," I said. "You just can't miss Cape Cod."

"Maybe we'll end up in Scituate," Milt suggested.

"Very funny," I told him, "but this is getting serious."

By chance, instead of searching straight ahead, I focused the binoculars just aft of the starboard beam. Barely visible on the edge of the horizon, I saw the tall tower of the Pilgrim Monument.

"We're way outside the cape," I said. "We've missed it completely. Give me the wheel, Carl. We have a long tack back."

As Carl left his position, I glanced at the compass. When he moved away, the compass rose swung 30 degrees to the right.

"Come back here a minute, Carl," I said.

He returned to his position and the compass rose swung 30 degrees to the left.

"That damn leg of yours is magnetized," I said. "No wonder we're twenty-five miles to the east of the cape. From now on you stay away from that wheel or we'll end up in Bermuda."

Each degree of compass error results in being one mile off course for every sixty miles sailed. We had traversed about one hundred twenty miles from our departure point and, because Carl had steered more than his fair one-quarter of the time, our error was about twenty-five miles. While it lengthened our voyage by a few hours, no one teased Carl. After all having a magnetized leg is not funny.

The compass was also the central figure on my longest passage. For two years, *Shag* had been based in the Virgin Islands, and on Good Friday, 1970, she started the long homeward bound voyage with Miami as the immediate destination. I had prepared *Shag* for her journey with great care. Food and beer in plenty had been stowed aboard. Sails, sheets and halyards checked. Although I anticipated a small role for the engine in the trade wind sailing, it, too, had received a thorough inspection. So I was well-satisfied that sunny morning in Red Hook on St. Thomas as my three crew members came aboard. All three were young professionals. They were engaged in delivering boats from manufacturers' yards on the mainland to augment the fleet for bareboat charters in the islands. They had just completed a delivery, so my return voyage exactly fitted their needs for transportation back to the States. Jack was to function as navigator, for I had not taken a celestial sight since my days in the Navy and never from a small boat. Bruce and Will split duties as deck hands, sometime cooks, and watch standers.

We bid farewell to our friends at the marina, cast off from the dock, and powered out of the harbor, setting the sails as we faced into the moderate trade wind. We swung off to the small islands just north of St. Thomas, and within a half an hour we were in position to take our navigational departure from the farthest out island. We streamed the patent log and set the watches. We had decided to have one man on watch for two-hour periods, with each taking a four-hour watch at noon so that the duty periods advanced by one each day. This system gave each of us six hours off for each two hours on. Bruce drew the first watch, sat behind the wheel, and pulled the binnacle cover back so he could see the compass.

"What the hell is the matter with this compass?" he exploded.

We all peered over his shoulder and watched the compass rose bounce 45 degrees on either side of north each time *Shag* hit a wave. In my two years in the fog-free Virgins, I had never once looked at the compass, for each island is easily in sight of another. In my preparations for the voyage, I had checked everything else but, unaccountably, I had not even glanced at the compass. Watching the compass's gyrations Jack said, "The dampening fluid has either leaked out or evaporated. I guess all we can do is go into Puerto Rico and get it repaired or get another. Do you have another on board?"

I admitted I did not have a spare. The long voyage was hardly off to an auspicious start.

"What is the dampening fluid?" I asked.

Jack answered, "I believe it is alcohol."

"Well, we have four bottles of gin and a couple of bottles of vodka on board. How about filling it with liquor? It's almost pure alcohol and it's colorless."

Jack replied, "We can try it, but finding Miami without a reliable compass won't be any fun at all."

We removed the compass from the binnacle, unscrewed the filler cap from the side, and through a small funnel poured a quart of Tanqueray gin into it.

"That's one thirsty compass," I remarked as the last of the gin dribbled into the bowl.

We put the instrument back into the binnacle, and Jack took some bearings on the still visible land. The compass had stopped its gyrations, and while the gin was cloudy through the glass, the compass rose was clearly visible.

"We'll find out how accurate it is when we take sights tomorrow," Jack said. "If it's way off, we'll have to either correct for it or make some harbor for repairs."

A star fix at dawn disclosed that our dead reckoning position was very close to our actual location so the compass was accurate. But the fluid level was already beginning to drop in the bowl.

"He wants another drink," I said.

"He's a damn bar fly," Jack observed.

Another gin bottle came out, and we poured half its contents into the bowl.

"That ought to keep him for twenty-four hours," I said. "I just hope the liquor lasts."

It did. Each noon, the compass received his gin ration as bottles were thrown overboard every second day. On the seventh day, after the most glorious sail downwind at top speed before the easterly trade winds, we entered Biscayne Bay and raised the yellow "Q" flag to our spreaders to summon the customs' authorities. Soon after we tied up to the Miami Marina, an inspector came aboard.

"How much liquor do you have on board?" he inquired.

"Not as much as we had when we left St. Thomas," I told him.

"Drink a lot on the trip, eh?" he asked.

"We didn't but the compass did," I told him and explained the dipsomaniacal symptoms of our navigational aid. "We still have half a quart left. Join us for a drink to the compass."

The inspector glanced at his watch. It was three minutes after five in the afternoon.

"I've been off duty three minutes," he said. "I'll join you."

We toasted the compass and speculated as to how it would have liked vodka if the length of our trip had forced us to substitute for its regular ration of gin.

9

Going Aground

A succinct slogan frames a warning for Merchant Marine skippers: "If you hit the bottom, you hit the beach." Translated into landlubber language it means that if for any reason a vessel goes aground, the skipper will never have another sea command. The Navy is equally harsh, and a naval officer who grounds his vessel can look forward to pushing papers around a desk, probably in some undesirable spot like the Aleutian Islands, for the rest of his truncated professional career. Fortunately, no equally harsh penalty results from grounding a privately owned pleasure boat, for if it did my sailing career would have ended early and often. I am an expert on going aground. I have beached every boat I have ever owned, never on purpose. I have gone aground in my familiar home harbor, in harbors often visited without incident, and in totally strange harbors entered for the first time. I have been aground in waters ranging from Nova Scotia and New Brunswick all the way down the eastern seaboard and including the Bahamas and the Virgins. I have gone aground under sail, under power, and even at anchor. I have gone aground alongside a dock, and at a mooring. I have gone aground in the middle of a delineated channel exactly equidistant between the red and black buoys which marked it. My logbooks record one stretch of nine consecutive days the first time I cruised in Chesapeake Bay when I went aground for varying periods at least once every day. I recall that on the tenth day of that cruise, when the anchor was snugly down in a beautiful Virginia river, I kissed Jane with unaccustomed warmth, at least for a daytime kiss in public view. "What's that for?" my surprised mate inquired. "We didn't go aground once today," I told her.

When I recall these countless groundings have all been accomplished in boats that drew six feet or less, it seems a record of unequalled incompetence. Yet miraculously, I have never damaged a boat by grounding it. After nearly a year of sailing *Shag,* we returned her to her builder's yard in Southwest Harbor, Maine. I asked Henry Hinckley to haul *Shag* and make the repairs necessary to restore her to her original splendid condition. Henry asked me to give him a brief history of my experience with the boat to help him draw up the required job orders.

"Well, Henry," I told him, "I'd be less than forth-right if I failed to tell you that I've taken her aground a good many times in the Bahamas, in Florida, in the Intracoastal Waterway, and even here in Maine."

He said, "You know there are people who never take their boats aground."

"There are?" I responded in wonderment.

"Yep," he replied, "They never go anywhere."

The only grounding in which I was involved on any boat that attracted public attention, or at least press attention, occurred with *Rose II*. The newspaper clips tell the story.

Hide Identity of Marooned Youths' Girl

Marblehead, Sept. 1—The age of adventure and chivalry is not dead. Four young men of the exclusive Marblehead Neck colony have proven this.

The young men in question are Richard Thayer, Robert Phillips, Winfield Ware and George Kirstein and they proved the age of adventure still lived when they piled their yacht up on a ledge at the entrance to Marblehead Harbor and were marooned there for hours with the surf threatening to pound the boat to pieces.

The chivalry end of the story comes in with the fact that the young men were accompanied by a young lady. The quartet banded together to save her name from becoming known and after hours on the ledge, when the party was finally rescued, the girl was spirited away and no amount of sleuthing could unearth the identity of the maid.

The boat, a 21-foot sloop, grounded off Baker's Island and after some time the predicament of the five was noted by other yachtsmen. The Humane Society was notified and one of their rescue boats put out for the ledge.

The rescue boat stood by until the rising tide finally lifted the sloop off the rocks. The boat was towed to the float of the Corinthian Yacht Club where the girl was quickly taken indoors and later was taken away in an automobile.

I have no recollection whatever of the identity of the girl nor of our motivations protecting her name from the shame of being with four boys in a boat, lying over on its side on a rock, waiting for the tide to float off. However, if her secret is ever discovered after these forty years, I can assure anyone interested that her virtue could not have been safer had she been confined in a convent.

Although my subsequent groundings have never again attracted the attention of the press, a number of them have drawn the amused attention of multitudes of passing boatmen and spectators on shore. It is bad enough to go aground, privately and unnoticed in some hidden river bend or isolated cove. At the very least, shame for the faulty pilotage punishes the erring skipper. But when the vessel grounds high and dry in front of God and everybody, public ignominy adds to personal humiliation.

The largest crowd I ever attracted to one of my many displays of incompetence was at my third entrance to Atlantic City, New Jersey. No harbor on the whole east coast is easier to enter than Atlantic City. A well-buoyed channel marks the path up the Abescon inlet, and the snug Atlantic City basin is open and clearly visible as you approach. Boat traffic is heavy because fish flourish in these waters, and multitudes of fishermen pursue them in powerboats. In 1962 on my first cruise to Chesapeake Bay I had negotiated this harbor both going and returning without incident. But on a return cruise the following year I displayed my skills.

On a lovely May day we entered the familiar inlet and proceeded under power to the mouth of the harbor. As we swung left to enter the basin which contains a huge state-operated marina, I saw a big black spar on our right side.

"They must have dredged a new channel," I said to Jane. "I don't remember that spar way over on the right."

"I think we went to the left of it last year," she said. "There doesn't seem to be any room to the right of it."

"Well, it's black," I said, "and that means we leave it on the left side entering."

I slowed *Skylark* down, but we were still going at a fair clip as I passed the black spar close aboard on my left. Then *Skylark* came to an abrupt halt as her keel grounded on a mud bank.

"I guess we should have left it on the other side," Jane said.

"I don't understand," I replied as I threw the engine in reverse to try to back off. "It sure as hell is black."

The tide was falling, and our efforts to refloat were unavailing. In a few minutes, a launch from the nearby Coast Guard station approached.

"Are you aground?" the petty officer who was steering the boat asked.

It was the first time we were to hear that oft-repeated question although the answer seemed all too obvious.

"We are indeed. Why in the world did you guys put a black spar way over here if the channel is on the other side?"

"Oh, it isn't a black spar," he replied cheerfully.

Skylark *aground in Chesapeake Bay, 1962.*

"We just smeared tar on it as a preservative. You can see it has a red light at the top."

I inspected the misleading aid to navigation and saw for the first time the small red light which perched unlit in daytime on top of the buoy.

"Do you want a line?" the coxswain asked. "We may be able to pull you off."

"No thanks. I'm scared we'll damage the rudder if you pull us off backward. We'll wait a few hours for the tide to come in."

It was perhaps four in the afternoon when we went aground. The sportfishermen began returning to the harbor around five. Each passing boat gaped at us, and then the crews broke into broad grins as they saw our predicament. One out of every three repeated the coxswain's question, "Are you aground?" At first, I answered politely, "Yes we are," but as the hours wore on, I tried different responses.

"No, we're moored here for the night," or "Why do you ask?" "We're on a scientific expedition to explore mud banks" or finally "What does it look like?"

Just why being asked a question that should require no answer is so irritating I do not know. However, I suggest that any motorist, pulled over to the side of the road and changing a tire after suffering a puncture, would explode if a passerby, viewing the scene, asked "Did you have a flat tire?"

In addition to the passing boats, a large group gathered on the dock of the nearby state marina, and by breaking into uproarious laughter, signified their amusement at an idiot who could go aground outside a clearly delineated channel. In addition, the personnel of the Coast Guard station seemed to be pointing out our plight to new recruits as a horrible example of the stupidity for which they were called upon, under more dire circumstances, to risk their lives.

We suffered for about four hours before the incoming tide freed us. Feeling sheepish, we approached the marina for a berth assignment. Even the dockmaster laughed at us as he took our lines.

While this grounding incident was my most embarrassing, the longest one occurred later on the same cruise. Chesapeake Bay offers countless opportunities to go aground, both because much of it is shallow, and because its many rivers offer beautiful invitations for exploration while the flow of the water constantly creates shifting shoals. Charts cannot remain accurate, and, although the government frequently dredges, silting builds new and uncharted mud banks even on the edges of marked channels.

We had had a beautiful sail, running before a strong wind up the narrow winding Chester River on the bay's eastern shore. We even found a marina which offered shower baths to mariners for a modest fee, so we availed ourselves of this welcome facility. In the late afternoon we began our return under power. We had encountered no difficulty sailing up the river between the many buoys which marked the channel. However, soon after we had started down, instead of staying in midstream, I came very near a buoy marking the edge of the channel. *Skylark* came to the now familiar squishy halt that signified a soft mud bottom.

"Gosh, we're on the channel side, aren't we?" I asked Jane.

"It looks to me," she said "as though we're awfully close to the edge. I guess the mud has banked even in the channel."

We tried all the usual techniques to free ourselves.

We reversed the motor. No luck. By using "Judas," I took an anchor well out into the channel, and tried to pull *Skylark* off by taking tension on the anchor rope. The anchor moved, *Skylark* did not.

"What's the tide doing?" asked Jane who was by now well experienced in grounding.

I examined the volume of tide tables published annually by the government.

"This one is really a beauty. We went aground just thirty minutes after high tide. We have more than eleven hours to wait before she will float off."

"It's going to be a long night," Jane said. "We might as well have a drink."

The tidal range in the Chesapeake is relatively small, about three feet on each rise and fall. As the tide retreated, *Skylark* leaned further and further over on her side as the water withdrew its support. By midnight, at low tide, she was canted over at a 45 degree angle. There was nothing we could do, so we crawled into our tilting bunks, wedged ourselves in, and went to sleep. When we awoke at dawn, the incoming tide had already floated *Skylark* off her muddy bed, and she was once again upright, swinging to the anchor we had put out in the channel. We examined the spot of our grounding.

"I still think we were in the channel," I said.

"Maybe we were," my mate replied, "but I think we would be a lot better off if we gave the buoys a wide berth from now on."

There could be no argument with this dearly purchased wisdom.

The Atlantic City grounding was the most humiliating, the Chester River one the longest, but by all odds the most uncomfortable, even painful one occurred in the upper reaches of the beautiful St. John River in

Canada's province of New Brunswick. This river emp-
ties into the Bay of Fundy at the large industrial city of
St. John, and is navigable along its winding course for
nearly one hundred miles to the provincial capital of
Fredrickton. Tributaries, bays, and lakes lead into it so
that weeks can be spent on the river without exhaust-
ing all possible exploration. The huge tides from the
Bay of Fundy enter the river, but are met and forced
back by the flowing current, so that from about forty
miles above the mouth there is no tidal action. The
Canadian government issues detailed charts of the
river, but their accuracy, through no fault of the
meticulous surveyors, is extremely undependable. Not
only does the river flow alter the formation of the
bottom, but if the region is blessed with heavy spring
rains, the river bed is deepened. We cruised there for
the first time after the driest spring in the records of
New Brunswick.

When we entered the busy port of St. John, we had
been signalled from the shore to tie up alongside the
pilot boat, so that immigration authorities and
custom's inspectors could clear us to enter Canada.
After clearance, one of the harbor pilots who guided
huge seagoing vessels into the frequently fog enshrouded harbor, kindly volunteered to guide us
through the reversible falls which guard the river
entrance. When the thirty-foot tide in the Bay of
Fundy is high, sea water pours into the river creating a
falls going upstream. When the tide is low, the river
pours its own fresh water and returns the seawater in
an enormous cascade, which viewed from the shore at
full flow looks like a miniature Niagara. For half an
hour or so on each tidal cycle, the level of the sea
exactly equals the level of the river, and vessels can
then proceed in still water up the river. Bruce Camp-

bell, our pilot, was himself a boat owner and a member of the local yacht club. After he had selected the correct moment to traverse the falls, he marked our charts, crossing out shallow tributaries caused by the paucity of spring rain. He warned us we might go aground early and often if we wandered out of the deepest branches of the river.

We gained confidence in the days that followed, for no mishap befell us. Salmon leapt clear of the water as we passed through rocky gorges, along pasture land that bordered the river, and past pretty little villages with high white church steeples standing above neat frame houses. We sailed to the very end of the navigable channel at Fredrickton, and on return, we chose alternate branches of the river which we had not explored on our way up. It was in one of these narrow tributaries that we grounded in the muddy bottom. We were above any tidal influence, thus entirely dependent on our own efforts. We were four men, so we had little doubt that we had sufficient strength to free *Skylark* and back her into deeper water. We put out two anchors, one astern so that we could pull the boat backward, and the other we placed to the side and attached to the mainsail halyard, leading to the top of the mast. The idea was that by taking up on the halyard, *Skylark* would be tilted through the leverage of the mast, thus making her shallower.

It was a very hot, sunny afternoon, and we were all in bathing suits. Everything was in readiness for our effort, anchors attached, winches manned, the engine running in reverse and *Skylark* tilted to the side, when the flies discovered us. Large, greenheaded deer flies, they were the kind that not only bit and itched but drew blood at each successful attack. And they came by the thousands. With all eight of our hands engaged in our two-anchor effort to free *Skylark*, we could not fight back. For nearly an hour the flies feasted on our perspiring bodies without hindrance. The anti-insect spray we had aboard merely whetted their appetites. *Skylark*'s ten tons had to be pulled each inch of the way off the mud bank, and she was reluctant to leave her soft resting place. Anchors had to be reset and pulled anew. All the while, the flies attacked. For no reason we could understand, once *Skylark* floated free, the swarms of flies disappeared leaving four itching, bleeding, sweating victims to rejoice at their departure.

While Chesapeake Bay offers splendid opportunities for grounding, and any river with a fast-flowing current presents numerous possibilities, the unsurpassed area to practice the various techniques for freeing a boat from her embraces with the land is the whole area of the Bahamas. The entire island chain is laced with huge shoals of fine shifting coral sand, and coral heads present their bulk on the bottom inviting keels to hit them. Added to these attractions are the most inaccurate charts I have ever encountered, depicting islands where none exist and showing open water where a sandy cay is in clear view. Pilotage, for the most part, is accomplished by staring at the crystal clear water and estimating by eye whether the passage just ahead is deep enough to accommodate your vessel. Until one becomes skilled at this translation of water color into probable depth, groundings are inevitable and frequent. Even after one has learned that blue purple water is deep, whitish water denotes a sand bottom of sufficient depth, greenish black water is shallow and grassy, and black spots are coral heads, the groundings continue but with less frequency.

When the depth is on the borderline between

navigable and impossible, a sounding pole a little longer than the draft of the vessel is more useful than a conventional lead line. The depth can be tested with a pole much more quickly than retrieving the lead line and casting it anew. Fathometers are virtually useless for they record depth under the boat rather than ahead of it. These electronic depth finders clearly record insufficient depth when you are already aground, but, by that time, you are well aware of your plight without the instrument's revolving light. The sun is the most important aid to navigation, because when it is high it emphasizes the varying depths of the water by coloring the sea. Sailing at night is courting disaster, and, if the sun is in your eyes early in the morning or late at night, it loses its beneficial effect, as it does when it is covered with clouds. Anyone who fears grounding rather than just hating it should stay well away from the Bahamas.

We grounded the very first day we arrived in the islands and on the last day before our departing, as well as countless times in between. Our first brush with the sandy bottom was an insignificant touch as we approached the officially manned harbor of entry on Cat Cay, but our last grounding came nearer to resulting in tragedy than any other in which I have been involved. We had determined to return to Florida from the northernmost harbor in the chain on Grand Bahama Island. The direct approach from Abaco to Grand Bahama is across the Little Bahama Bank. Charts of this bank show depths between nine and twelve feet with occasional six-foot spots. As *Shag* draws only four feet, we felt that the direct line across the bank was feasible. After an uneventful sail of some fifteen miles, we went aground within sight of our destination, perhaps five miles from the harbor. Looking down at the clearly visible bottom, we could see that the water on all sides of us was about the same depth, so that there was no point in struggling to extricate ourselves as it would merely result in fruitlessly bumping over the bottom.

It was early afternoon when we grounded and the tide was halfway out and ebbing. In short, we all knew we had about nine hours to wait before we floated free. There was no point in fretting; we behaved as if we were anchored in a safe harbor, reading, playing card games, and talking. *Shag* stayed on an even keel so shipboard life was normal. At six o'clock in the evening all four of us went down to the cabin to prepare supper. Although the tide was at dead low level, *Shag* seemed steady as a rock in an absolutely upright position. Suddenly a shift in our weights as we moved around the cabin threw the boat from her upright position where she had been balancing on her narrow keel over onto her beam ends, so that her mast now pointed at 45 degrees rather than at the perpendicular.

Jane was sitting on the side which ended up being the low side so she barely moved. Milton, my companion, and I were already sitting behind the upraised table and so we were thrown a few inches before the table checked us. But Milton's wife, Mary, was flung the whole width of the boat with great force, and her head and shoulders struck the wood panelling opposite where she had been sitting. She was nearly knocked unconscious, but somehow a kind fate determined that no damage beyond vivid black and blue bruises resulted. Five hours later as the tide was nearly high, we powered in the darkness of the night to deeper water and anchored. The next day, also at high tide, we left the bank and entered the harbor at West End. But we had learned one final lesson about grounding—

namely, if, by chance, a grounded boat stays on an even keel when the water withdraws its buoyant support, move around the vessel with the utmost caution.

Grounding is a little like the other hazard of sailing, running in fog. Anyone who says they enjoy either of these experiences is a liar or a fool. But both hazards can be surmounted by varying combinations of luck, experience, and skill; and all who follow the sea for pleasure or profit will encounter both at some time in his voyages.

10

Lessons of Fog

Early in my cruising career, we just refused to sail in fog. We had no experience with running blind, and we were not yet aware of the frequency of fog's occurrence on the Maine coast. On one three-week vacation, we determined to explore the beauties of that area. In less than a week of fine weather, we got as far as York Harbor, and then the fog came in. It was a typical New England hot spell with the temperature in Boston staying in the high nineties, ideal conditions for the optimum manufacture of fog. For two days we stayed on the boat, swinging to the strong harbor tides, completely unable to even see one hundred yards to where a huge hotel dominates the landscape. Then

Rose became so uncomfortable, wet, and clammy that we took a room in a boarding house.

Each morning we would rise hopefully, look out the window, and see the swirling clouds of grey mist. A mile inland, the weather was hot and sunny. It was maddening. Day after day of our limited vacation evaporated because of the blinding muck. York Harbor is a nice village, an unpretentious summer resort. Our lodgings were comfortable, the food and wine were good. Yet I grew to hate York Harbor with a hatred I still cherish. For ten days, which represented more than half of our vacation, the fog cloaked even the narrow harbor entrance. At least twice, we made a start, but could not even see the first channel buoy and returned.

One day I was idling on the gasoline dock watching the lobster boats pursue their familiar routines. From out of the fog, a yawl under power ghosted to the dock and tied up.

"Thick out there?" I asked.

"Can't see a damn thing," the yawl's owner told me.

"Where did you come from?" I inquired.

"Shelburne, Nova Scotia."

"My heavens," I said. "Were you really aiming for York Harbor?"

"Sure," he laughed. "We haven't seen anything since we left Cape Sable, but with the direction finder we didn't have too much trouble."

"That's my boat over there," I said pointing, "but we don't sail in fog."

"We don't like it much ourselves," he said, "but we decided a long time ago if we were going to sail on this coast, we'd better get used to it."

And so we have.

There are various textures of fog ranging all the way

108

from the fair weather haze that is typical when the prevailing summer southwester fans the New England coast to the pea soup variety that abounds in Nova Scotia and even hides the mast from a viewer ten feet away in the cockpit. The further east one sails on the coast of Maine the more splendid, thick, and gooey is the fog. The Bay of Fundy very nearly rivals Nova Scotia for the quality, thickness, and invisibility of its fog, but any impartial judge would have to award the prize to the waters between Cape Sable and the Bras d'Or Lakes on Nova Scotia's south coast.

I discussed the manufacture of fog with my crew as we sailed these waters. We agreed that small dwarfs, all bearded, and each at least one thousand years old, man the fog machines. The leader has charge of thickness and his assistants aid with color and degree of wetness.

"Put more purple in, Jake," orders the head dwarf, and obligingly Jake adds that color.

"Green, Bill," and Bill mixes his ingredient.

These dwarfs have great skill, and we came to believe that they serve an apprenticeship of at least a thousand years during which time it is their duty to harden the rocks which form the coastal ledges. Their success in this endeavor is rewarded when they advance to the fog machine itself and are able to contemplate the disasters which their earlier work assures.

Most daytime port-to-port sails in the fog are not particularly memorable although each has the tension of proceeding blindfolded. Before departing, I lay out accurate compass courses between sound-making buoys and measure exactly the distance between them. If tidal current is a factor, I try to estimate its effect on the various courses, and allow for the drift in my plotting. Instead of a stopwatch to time the expected runs between the buoys, I use a cooking timer which rings when the time estimated to run the distance has elapsed. In addition, we trail a Walker log which shows the distance run through the water. When the timer rings and the log shows we have run the distance to the buoy, everyone listens. Most times someone will hear the noise, and we follow hand signals pointing at the sound until the buoy is in sight. Nine times out of ten, this system works effectively. In theory, it should be infallible. Several factors modify the theory when it is put to practice. Firstly, no one can steer a small boat without deviating from a straight line, so the best one can hope for is to end up near enough the objective to hear it and then follow the sound until the navigational aid is in sight. But, in calm weather, bell and whistle buoys, dependent on wave action to fulfill their function, ring or blow infrequently. Furthermore, many buoys mark shoals on one side, so to be safe one must set a course near enough to hear them but far enough away from the shoal side to assure safety.

Perhaps the most frustrating factor of all is that noise does not behave normally in fog. First the sailor hears a buoy and heaves a sigh of relief. Then he cannot hear it. Then faintly it sounds to the right. The skipper aims for it. Now it is on the left. Then it fades. Sometimes the buoy looms up next to the boat, looking like a skyscraper, and the sound on the side from which the vessel approaches is virtually inaudible, yet once past the buoy the noise on the far side seems deafening. In addition, the horns on passing vessels may be mistaken for whistle buoys with extremely unpleasant results. There is no doubt about it, sailing in fog diminishes the pleasure. Indeed, it is no fun at all.

Sometimes luck plays a larger role than skill. With

Jane as crew, we left Stonington homeward bound one summer morning. The haze was heavy and the fog was threatening. Conditions were just right for its appearance, with a hot spell on the land and the wind gathering force from the southwest. Fortunately, visibility was up to two hundred yards as we negotiated the complex, multibuoyed channel through Fisher's Island Sound; but, just off New London, the fog thickened and visibility was reduced to zero. We were not unduly concerned because we knew precisely where we were when visibility was lost and because Long Island Sound is wide and has few obstructions to navigation, at least in the middle. The only factor that upsets calculations in this area is the extremely strong tidal current. Billions of gallons of water pour from the Atlantic into the narrow entrances to the sound, causing currents that run to four and five knots. For the most part, the current flows dependably west on the flood and east on the ebb, but there are counter currents and back eddies near the land. Our first objective was a complex of sound-making buoys off the mouth of the Connecticut River. We knew if we missed a bell, we would come to a whistle. Beyond both and inshore, Saybrook lighthouse loudly brays its warning from the breakwater at the river's mouth.

About an hour after we began to run blind, an object loomed up just ahead of us. It was a tiny Sunfish, those popular single-sailed little craft that exist in vast quantities near every yachting center. As *Skylark* was being propelled by the engine, I turned it off and yelled at the bathing suit clad sailor of the cockleshell.

"Are you all right?" Here he was out in the middle of Long Island Sound, unable to see, and in a vessel about the size of a bathtub.

"I'm fine," he called back.

"Know where you are?" I persisted.

"Sure," he called back with assurance. Then with a note of warning in his voice, he asked, "Hey, Captain, you know where you are?"

"I think so," I said. "I'm about a mile off the beach near Saybrook."

"Captain, you're near Saybrook all right, but you are about fifty yards from the beach. You can hear the bathers talking."

With the engine quiet, we could hear children's voices very near us.

"Thanks," I called out as I turned *Skylark*'s bow directly away from the danger.

"The tide must have carried us in," I explained to my startled wife.

"Lucky you decided to help that Sunfish," Jane said. "It gave him a chance to rescue us."

Port-to-port sailing in fog is replete with uncertainties despite the frequent occurrence of buoys and other aids to navigation, but it is uneventful compared to making a landfall on a strange coast, shrouded by fog, after a long sea passage. In the summer of 1953, *Skylark* manned by an all-male crew, left Marblehead bound for Shelburne, Nova Scotia, on a typically hazy day with the wind a gentle southwester. It was delightful sailing on a course east by one half south which permitted a spinnaker run on the direct line to Cape Sable. A thundersquall passed over us from the west about sundown, but, after a couple of hours of heavy rain accompanied by loud thunder crashes and little wind, the night became beautiful with a large moon shining though the clearing weather.

Halfway across, right on the course, a single whistle buoy, Townsend Ledge, keeps a lonely vigil. We

112

hoped, although we hardly expected, to sight this pinpoint in the ocean. Soon after dawn, we did spy the lonely sentinel and congratulated ourselves on our excellent helmsmanship. Oh, we were mariners par excellence. The clear weather, the soft following wind, the smooth sea, and the sun burning down added to our euphoria. The difficulties we had anticipated, problems of navigation, the uncertainties of Fundy's tides were all illusory. There was nothing to it; a child could make this passage in a canoe.

Then at sunset, the fog came in. At first it was wispy, but, after the sun went down, it settled into a heavy, impenetrable blindfold which made the classic words "ceiling zero, visibility zero" a concrete reality. We were not unduly apprehensive. According to our dead reckoning, we were still forty or fifty miles from the Nova Scotia coast. There was not the slightest purpose in trying to peer ahead through the fog curtain; nevertheless all four of us stared endlessly ahead of *Skylark*'s bow.

Just after midnight we heard the faint sound of a fog horn almost dead ahead.

"That's all we need now," I said. "Some ship wandering around out here on a converging course."

"It's still a long way away," Mike said, and there was no question that the faint sound of the powerful horn was at a good distance. But, as we held our course, the periodic blasts from the fog horn became increasingly loud.

"He must be on the opposite course," I guessed. "Probably going from Halifax to Boston."

"I don't know where he is going," Mike replied, "but I sure don't like this. He's getting too close."

I didn't like it either. In the blackness of the night with the fog obscuring all vision, it was clear the ship

113

was on a converging course, and from the volume of sound coming from its blasting horn it was easy to surmise it was a very big ship indeed.

"Let's get the hell out of here," I said. "Turn her around on the reciprocal course." The helmsman turned the wheel and *Skylark* spun around in her own wake.

Like the rest of us, Martin who had volunteered to act as navigator had been listening intently to the ever loudening horn. When *Skylark* was steady on the course which if pursued would lead back to Marblehead, he said, "You know that horn blows at precise intervals. No ship would be that exact. I think it's a lighthouse on the land."

I laughed. "If we're where we think we are, there isn't a lighthouse within thirty miles."

Martin insisted and after a pause went below to get a stopwatch. For a period of five minutes we timed the horn. It blew exactly at intervals of once every fifty seconds. We searched the chart for lighthouses within fifty miles that were marked as having fog horns.

"It's got to be Seal Island," Martin said. "I'll check the Canadian Light List for its characteristic."

Sure enough our research disclosed that the Seal Island horn blew every fifty seconds.

"My God," I said, "we're twenty miles up in the Bay of Fundy, and we ought to be at least ten miles out to sea from Cape Sable. We've been sucked up into the Bay by thirty miles."

I drew a circle about five miles wide on the chart fairly near Seal Island and then plotted a safe new course to take us around Cape Sable.

Martin said, "I'll get out the radio direction finder and see if I can pick up any marine station."

I told him that I did not have much faith in the

114

instrument because they were never accurate to within three to five degrees, but that if he wanted to play with it any help it gave would be appreciated.

We sailed on the new course until long after the fog had shifted color from ebony black to deep gray, disclosing that somewhere in the atmosphere above us dawn had come. The color of the fog made little difference; we could hardly see the bow of the boat thirty-five feet from the cockpit where we were sitting.

Martin succeeded in getting some bearings on the direction finder, and they merely confirmed our guess that at last we were outside of the unseen Cape Sable. At noon after sailing perhaps ten hours on our safety course, I said, "We have to be clear of it now. Let's head in for the land and hope we hear something before we hit it."

Within an hour we did hear something. Very faintly a foghorn was blasting its message. Out came the stopwatch again to time the periods between the blasts. Martin identified the sound as coming from the Rosemay lighthouse at the mouth of the Shelburne River.

"Let's aim for it," I said. "Once we see it, all we have to do is follow the shore up the river. The fog ought to clear over the land, and we're in like Flynn."

We altered our course a few degrees one way or the other to keep the ever increasing noise of Rosemay Light constantly on our bow. We guessed it was a few miles away when we first heard it, but we badly underestimated. We sailed at a good speed toward the noise for at least two hours which covered ten to twelve miles. Finally the noise of the blast became so loud that it offended our ears each time it repeated its throaty bellow.

"You're going to run the damn thing down if you keep on," Mike, who was steering, warned.

"I'm going to see it before we turn for the river entrance," I told him. "I'll go on the bow, and when I see it you turn her fast for the new course up the bank of the river."

"I'll turn her fast all right," Mike assured me and added, "if we're not on the rocks."

I stood on the bow peering into the impenetrable fog.

The sound of the horn was by now so loud that *Skylark* trembled each time the deep-throated roar blasted. I could see nothing although we had to be within yards of the horn. I only hoped the lighthouse was situated near the rocky coast.

Then within twenty yards of the bow I saw breakers dashing on rocks, and the white column of the light-house faintly visible towering over us.

"Now," I screamed back at Mike.

Skylark whirled within her own length on to the new course that followed the bold shore of the Shelburne River. As the horn's blast receded in intensity, the fog lifted over the narrow river. The sun shone first through haze, then clearly as we ascended the six-mile-long river to Shelburne. Some fifty-two hours out of Marblehead, we anchored in sunny Shelburne Harbor.

Eighteen years later, I repeated the same voyage in *Shag*. Again, as we approached the estimated position of fog-shrouded Cape Sable, visibility was zero in the blackness of the night. But this time, around dawn, we chanced upon an entirely unexpected aid to navigation. Looming out of the fog only twenty yards or so from our course, a fishing boat was anchored. As I brought *Shag* nearer to the vessel, I could see the two fishermen handling their deep sea cod lines. I framed the question I intended to ask with some care because there is a classic joke about a similar encounter between a confused yachtsman and a lobster man off the coast of Maine.

Yachtsman: "Do you know where you are?"

Fisherman: "Nope."

Yachtsman: "What harbor are you from?"

Fisherman: "Tenant's Harbor."

Yachtsman: "Do you know the direction to Tenant's Harbor?"

Fisherman: "Nope."

Yachtsman: "You must be a damn fool not to know the direction of your home port."

Fisherman: "Mebbee. But I ain't lost and you are."

The secret, of course, is that the lobstermen know the exact location of their traps and proceed in thick fog without trouble from one to another. From the last trap of their route, they know the exact course back to port.

So I did not want to ask if the fishermen knew where they were. I presumed they did. As I came close to their boat, I called out, "Can you give me a bearing on anywhere?"

There was a momentary consultation between the two men. Then one yelled back.

"Cape Sable bears North-Northeast."

"Could you guess at the distance?" I called back.

"Oh, eleven, twelve miles, something like that."

"Thank you, captain," I yelled back as we drew beyond hearing range. From the position the fishermen gave us, I plotted the course to Lockport Harbor, and when the fog cleared near the land we could see that our course was correct, which proved that the position given us so hurriedly had been exactly accurate.

The contrast between these blind gropings for Cape Sable with our most recent effort over the same course was almost unbelievable. I had first encountered the

117

magic of radar in the Navy, and I had determined that, if the price and size of these electronic eyes were ever brought within reach, I would install one on *Shag*. Planning another run to the beautiful Canadian coast for 1975, I finally purchased one of these instruments. Yachtsmen who have used Loran, that other electronic miracle which pinpoints the boat's position practically at the turn of a knob, argue that it is more useful than radar. Radio direction finders, the only electronic aid to navigation a few years ago, are completely unsatisfactory so far as I'm concerned. At best, they furnish an estimated position that may be five or even ten miles from the boat's true location.

The weather was fair as we left Marblehead with a southeast wind which just allowed us to steer the easterly course for the cape. A lovely moonlit night followed the sunny afternoon, but I knew from past experience that with the wind anywhere in the south the fog would descend as we came nearer Nova Scotia. In the afternoon, it came in sure enough and the wind piped up to twenty-five or thirty knots. Under shortened sail of small jib and jigger, *Shag,* rail down in the cold water, made her best speed towards the hidden coast. As night came, rain came with it, and the wind shifted slightly so we were no longer able to point toward the cape. It was miserable. Cold, wet, with fog to the point of not being able to see the bow, we were three uncomfortable people.

"I am not going to tack out around the cape in this stuff," I told my crew. "We'll head for Yarmouth instead of trying to get around Cape Sable."

We had no idea exactly where we were, but the log we trailed indicated how far we had come from Marblehead. When our distance run indicated we were approaching the land, the waves diminished in height, a sure sign we were under the lee of the cape.

We switched on the radar, and it peered through the impenetrable fog and night showing nothing on its scope.

"We'll put it on its six-mile range and watch it."

Within an hour, the crew member who had drawn the assignment of watching the radar scope said, "I have land at six miles."

As we approached, the formation of the coast was outlined in the scope.

"There's an opening—looks like a harbor—10 degrees on our starboard side," my crew reported.

"Yarmouth," I said happily.

As we approached, we put our electronic eye on the three-mile range and more detail was disclosed.

"There is a buoy 5 degress to port, two and a half miles distant," reported my watcher.

Of course, we could see nothing, but our electronic eye gave us not only direction but the exact distance.

As we entered the harbor, one of my crew said, "That damn thing is magic."

And it is.

11

Those Inevitable Gear Failures

Man, being an essentially optimistic animal, does not anticipate that accidents or disasters will strike him. The novice sailor is a prime example of this euphoria. His boat is launched in the spring, and nothing, he thinks, will go wrong until it is hauled out in the fall. However, just as certain as the rise and fall of the tides, some part of the boat's equipment, will fail before the season ends. Boats are vulnerable to the action of wind and sea, and casualties will occur in direct proportion to the complexities built into each vessel. Hulls can leak, rigging can fail, spars can break, sails can tear, engines are subject to all the mechanical failures of land-based machines and a whole gamut of new complications caused by the corrosive action of salt water. Superlative maintenance reduces the number, seriousness, and frequency of casualties but no human action entirely eliminates their occurrence.

When I started sailing in the little 13-foot *Rose,* our equipment failures were self-inflicted. On one particularly memorable afternoon in my first year, we ventured forth from Marblehead harbor, crossed neighboring Salem Bay, and proceeded along the coast to Beverly's fine sand beaches, admiring the sunbathers and swimmers as we sailed on. With the bravado of Raleigh, with the adventurous spirit of Drake, with the skill of Magellan we explored this strange coast. Alas, we were suddenly transformed into Robinson Crusoes. We hit an outlying rock which lifted the rudder from the pintles attaching it to the stern. Unable to steer, we drifted broadside onto the beach among the numerous bathers who only a few moments before had been dazzled by our demonstration of nautical skill. It was humiliating. We telephoned the boatyard, relating the grim details of this disastrous shipwreck on a calm sunny summer afternoon, and in a couple of hours the yard's motorboat appeared. The workman asked, "Don't you keep an oar on that boat?" We did carry this primitive propulsion mechanism to assist in calms, so my answer was affirmative.

"You can steer these little things with an oar," he told us. It was our first lesson in making do with secondary equipment when a failure occurred.

When boats are more sophisticated, particularly when an engine is aboard, the chances for equipment failure multiply. The first summer we sailed *Tarheel* we received our indoctrination in engine mutiny. Our most distant point on that summer cruise was Nantucket. The approach to that old whaling harbor is a long and extremely narrow channel. We had a lovely sail in a typical summer southwest wind from Martha's Vineyard to reach Nantucket's outer buoy without incident. As the wind was blowing directly against us for the entrance, our plan was to drop the sails and use the engine for the last mile down the constricted channel. The idea was fine, but the Kermath withheld its approval.

I whirled that flywheel until the blisters on my hand wore off into raw flesh. The engine refused to roar. It was not the first time it had gone on strike, but this time we realized it was sick from some unknown illness which we could neither diagnose nor cure. We tacked up that narrow channel, going twenty-five yards in one direction, coming about, going twenty-five yards on the other tack, for what seemed hours. The tide was ebbing out of the harbor and our progress, as a result, was barely perceptible. At long last, after perhaps two hundred tacks, we entered the harbor at sundown.

The next morning, the first order of business was to persuade a mechanic to repair the engine. By eight o'clock I was ashore intent on my quest for a healer of mechanical maladies. Everywhere I turned, my search was frustrated. At the island's only boatyard I heard what was to become a refrain, "Our mechanic is down on the *Clio*." I tried several garages. Their mechanics were "down on the *Clio*." I was reduced to a survey of filling stations. Those few institutions which boasted a mechanic told me, "He is down on the *Clio*." I decided there must be a mechanics' convention taking place on the *Clio*, whatever or wherever she might be, and the place to go for a choice of engineering skills was this mystery vessel.

I walked along the docks, examining the names on the fishing vessels nested alongside each other. No *Clio*. At the end of the dock lay a beautiful 80-foot yawl. Her mahogany topsides were varnished, reflecting the sun from their spotless surfaces. Her decks were teak, scrubbed to a gleaming white. I examined the name on her counter and saw in gold leaf *Clio— Oyster Bay*. I marveled at the beauty and opulence of this luxurious yacht, as I came abreast of her main hatch. There, sitting on the hatch cover in a way that permitted him to peer below, obviously was the general of the army of mechanics who toiled below. The noise of hammering was loud and clear. Pipes, wheels, and other engine appurtenances were spread out in neat rows next to this overall-clad foreman, his hands besmeared with grease, a large greasy rag hanging out of one pocket of his overalls. I addressed him.

"I have to get a mechanic, and every mechanic on this island seems to be working on this boat."

"Yes," he said, "she burnt out her main bearing and the whole engine has to be moved to repair it."

"Well," I said, "I've got a little 2 cylinder, 2 cycle Kermath that won't start. I am pretty sure that there is nothing much the matter with it. A good man could probably fix it in five minutes, but I don't know enough to even find out what's wrong. Could you lend me one of these guys for half an hour? The owner of this boat will never miss him. He's probably playing tennis somewhere, anyway. And the man who can fix my engine will be doing me a big favor and earn a few extra bucks besides."

The foreman pulled out the rag and wiped the grease from his hands. He put his head down the hatch and called out to some invisible courier, "Tell my wife I've gone out in the harbor to look at the engine of a little boat."

I realized I had been addressing *Clio*'s owner, and I began to retreat.

"Maybe it does need a professional mechanic," I suggested. "Anyway, I wouldn't want to hold up repairs on this boat." My voice trailed off.

"Come on," he said. "Where's your dinghy?"

We rowed out to *Tarheel* in silence. I was apprehensive that my crew would greet us with queries about the competence of my mechanic and more particularly question the fee to be paid. I tried to pantomime for silence, but pantomime is difficult while rowing. We went below and viewed the recalcitrant engine.

"Turn it over," said the voice of authority. I whirled the flywheel.

"Once more," he said. Again a totally unresponsive whirl.

"The magneto is being short-circuited," he announced. "How do you stop this thing when it's running?" I demonstrated the push button on the shelf over the engine which it shared with the can containing gasoline to prime the cylinders.

"Move that gasoline container," he said.

"Move it?" I asked. "Move it where?"

"Just move it. Move it anywhere."

I moved the gasoline can six inches down the shelf.

"Now try it," he said.

For one of the few times in its life, the Kermath roared into activity on the first whirl.

Obviously, we had witnessed a miracle, but there had to be some explanation for this supernatural performance.

"There are only two things that can go wrong with these engines," he explained. "One is that they're not

124

getting enough gas; the other is that the magneto isn't functioning. I could tell by the sound, it was getting the gas, so it had to be the magneto. The snout of your gasoline can was crossing those two wires just as effectively as if you had been pushing the stop button. You could have cranked it a million times, and with that can where it was, you never would have started it."

"How in the world did you know what to do about a short-circuited magneto?" I asked in wonderment.

"Perhaps it's time to introduce myself," he said. "My name is Murray. I am the president of the Bosch Magneto Company."

"Good God," I exclaimed. "The president of a big American corporation who knows what the hell he is making."

He laughed. "Row me ashore," he said. "I only wish *Clio*'s engine was as simple to repair."

On a typical summer morning in any harbor on the coast, one or more boats needs repairs. A summer storm may have swept the harbor, or a motor may have refused to start, a sail may have torn the day before, or a compass, for some unaccountable reason, may have lost its accuracy. Cataloguing all possible ills that boats are heir to is impossible. In many ways, engine casualties are the most frustrating. The average sailor is not a mechanic, nor does he usually know even the basic cause of his auxiliary's recalcitrance. He goes ashore to seek out the assistance of the nearest mechanic who, of course, is busy. The mechanic is not only busy right now; he is tied up for days in advance on priority jobs where other owners, usually local boatmen who are his regular customers, are waiting impatiently for repairs. Nonetheless, often he can be prevailed upon to at least take a look on the owner's assurance that it will take an expert only seconds to diagnose the malady. Once aboard the boat, he is hooked, for engine problems fascinate a good mechanic as much as human frailties challenge a doctor.

Some engine casualties defy even the analysis of experts. *Skylark*'s motor was a 40 hp Gray gasoline engine respectfully called "Mr. Gray." Over our many years of association I became quite intimate with "Mr. Gray," and I could tell by his sounds when he did not feel well and usually what was wrong. Often a hammer blow on the appropriate section would cure his ailment; sometimes wires had to be dried. Occasionally impurities in his gasoline interfered with his digestive system, and his intestinal carburetor had to be taken apart and cleaned. But in the summer of 1953, he developed a new ailment that defied either diagnosis or cure. His symptoms were that he started with ease, ran smoothly as long as he idled, but as soon as he was called upon to speed up to his usual reliable cruising rate, he overheated. Red lights flashed on the instrument panel, steam emerged from his cooling system, and unless he was allowed to resume idling, he threatened suicide.

Various mechanics looked at him. They disassembled his cooling machinery which consisted of a rotary pump resembling a miniature water wheel. This device, made of a synthetic rubber compound, whirled around when the engine ran and furnished salt water to the pipes that kept "Mr. Gray's" temperature at normal. I got to know this piece of mechanism with a familiarity that led to every emotion but contempt. I respected that water pump; I admired it; but I came to hate it. Each time it was reassembled the current mechanic assured us that the engine was cured. "Mr. Gray" would start, idle satisfactorily while the mechanic was aboard, and promptly overheat as soon as the mechanic was safely out of sight. It was maddening.

We reached Marblehead from Mamaroneck with the help of following winds, and the occasional use of "Mr. Gray" at his best idling speed of two knots. At Marblehead the inevitable mechanic came aboard, performed the ritual of the water pump, pronounced "Mr. Gray" cured, and departed. We were bound across the Gulf of Maine to St. John, New Brunswick; and soon after the mechanic's departure we were on our way. No more than a mile out of Marblehead Harbor, the red lights flashed, and "Mr. Gray" screamed to be reduced in speed to his slowest. As soon as we accommodated him, we resumed our dawdling along at two knots.

For the next three days and nights, the weather was ideal. Sunny days, starlit nights, gorgeous summer weather. And not a breath of wind. The Gulf of Maine was like a frozen millpond. Only an occasional porpoise rippled the glassy surface. Hour after hour we crept along at two knots across the motionless sea. Finally outside St. John, the strength of the tide was greater than "Mr. Gray" could overcome, and we gladly accepted a tow from the pilot boat which was returning after a routine delivery of a pilot to an incoming ship. Tied up to a float in St. John's dirty harbor, we summoned a mechanic.

He was good, I'll say that for him. At least he tried some new measures. After performing the usual ritual of disassembling the water pump to no avail, he filled the cooling system with lye in the hope that whatever was clogging it would be dissolved. No improvement. For two days he labored while we peered over his shoulder. No improvement. His supervisor came. No improvement. Finally he took the water pump apart for the nth time. This time we examined the miniature water wheel with the greatest care. We noticed at long last that one of the perhaps one hundred tiny rubber blades had broken off. We then saw the little blade, no more than one-quarter inch in size floating in the cooling water. The mystery was solved. Every time the pump was turned up fast, the tiny piece of rubber was forced into the water pipe preventing the flow. At dead slow speed, there was not enough force to jam the outlet so the engine stayed cool. The cause of it all? Who knows? Perhaps some water had been left in the pump over the previous winter, frozen, and weakened that one tiny piece of rubber. Or maybe it was just born weak. In any event, the cause now known, we were soon on our way up the beautiful St. John River with "Mr. Gray" purring like a contented cat.

It is impossible to enumerate all of the things that can go wrong with a boat's engine, nor is this surprising when one compares the conditions under which a marine engine operates with those of the familiar trouble-free automobile. The automobile is used frequently, almost daily; the marine motor is used once in a while during the six summer and fall months. The auto engine copes only with fresh water for cooling; the marine engine has some salt water cooling, even when the radiator uses fresh water. An auto engine is kept mostly dry under its hood and housed in a garage; a marine engine is always damp and sometimes downright soaked. An automobile, for the most part, operates on level ground or a mild grade; marine engines are called on to perform gyrations that not even an armored tank could follow. Finally, mechanics who are capable of repairing the common ills of automobiles are available at service stations, garages, and, if all else fails, the service center of the agency where the car was purchased. Experts on marine engines are not all that abundant. There are many types of marine engines (gasoline, diesel, outboard, inboard, small and large), and compared to cars the average mechanic encounters relatively few of each kind. Automobile mechanics work twelve months a year on their specialty; in northern latitudes marine mechanics have a six month season, albeit a hectic one.

The result of all these factors is that frequently the true source of trouble is not diagnosed on the first effort. A succession of mechanics had cleaned the carburetor on "Mr. Gray" when the real problem was that the gasoline had water in it. After the tanks were pumped out, and clean fuel substituted, the carburetor performed perfectly. A series of mechanics at one hundred mile intervals worked on *Shag*'s diesel engine to ascertain what made it so unusually difficult to start. It was not until the machine refused even to budge that the fault was discovered in a leaking exhaust pipe which permitted salt water to penetrate the fuel supply. With a short sailing season, with even shorter vacations limiting the sailor's time, engine casualties which can consume frustrating days are always unwelcome.

Fortunately, only a few seasons are memorable because of a recurring casualty, but I remember the "Summer of the Toilet" well. Boat toilets are simple mechanisms which operate by a pump handle. Either a pedal may be pushed or a handle turned to allow sea water to enter the bowl, and, when pedal or handle are in normal position, working the pump handle discharges the contents into the sea. Year after year, a boat's toilet operates without trouble and with minimum attention. But one summer, after years of uncomplaining and efficient functioning, *Skylark*'s toilet revolted.

Its first symptoms were a continuing leak around the base which refused to stop regardless of our efforts to tighten the bolts securing the bowl to the deck. Then it wouldn't flush. One could pump one's heart out with the lever in the correct position and no sea water would enter. My theory of casualties is that if something does not work, try to fix it. If all that is accomplished is to ruin the gadget permanently or make its ultimate repair more difficult, what of it? It didn't work in the first place. On a particularly hot, humid afternoon I put my theory to practice by disassembling the toilet. A mounting pile of rubber washers, lead weighted valves, and nuts and bolts gathered around me. I examined all the working parts with care, but having no real idea of how the mechanism was supposed to work, I did not know exactly what I was looking for. At the end of a couple of hours, I had reassembled it in more or less the same way it had been before and hopefully pumped away. Nothing happened. No seawater entered no matter how persistently I manipulated the lever.

The immediate solution to this malfunction was to place a galvanized bucket in the toilet bowl thus making it more or less possible to use the seat in the way it was intended. Jane was unenthusiastic about this makeshift procedure. The galvanized bucket protruded above the level of the seat and besides, it had sharp edges where the handle was attached. She rarely threatened mutiny, but on this issue she left no doubt that either the toilet would be fixed or I could look for a new mate.

I telephoned a major yacht repair yard in Boothbay Harbor where we expected to be in about a week's time. I carefully gave the yard superintendent the specifications of the toilet, manufacturer's name, style number, and even the very hard-to-read serial number of the individual toilet. He assured me a replacement would be ordered from Boston and be ready for installation when we arrived.

Thus assured, Jane complained less about the bucket. When we reached Boothbay, we sought out the superintendent. He informed us that the manufacturer had long since discontinued this particular model. He offered to personally inspect the offender to see what repairs were possible or to see if any current model could replace our antique. Of course, none did. A workman disassembled the mechanism again and reassembled it. He worked the pump handle and a grudging trickle of sea water entered. He pronounced it fixed. For two days the toilet cooperated in a halfhearted way. Then it quit.

We were only a week away from our home port so by persuasion, promises of future repair, and blandishments I persuaded Jane to stay aboard. A week later about ten miles before we reached Mamaroneck, I asked Jane to steer. I went below and closed the toilet's sea cocks. I unbolted the base and unhitched the pipes. Having freed the instrument, I struggled with it through the cabin and up the hatch ladder. Jane viewed this performance with questioning eyes.

"What in the world are you doing?" she asked.

"I'm going to throw the son of a bitch overboard," I told her and I did.

The range of casualties is infinite. Threading the maze of lobster pots entering a Maine harbor, a line becomes entangled in the propellor. It may bend the shaft or nick the propellor. Electronic gear becomes damp and won't work. The bilge pump, for some inexplicable reason, refuses to function. Cleats pull out of the deck under unusual strains. Winches freeze from lack of lubrication. The catalogue of things that can go wrong is endless and starts at the bow and goes all the way to the stern. The universal lesson, always learned the hard way, is that the unanticipated failure can be expected at any time.

12

Chartering

Two logical reasons exist for chartering boats. First, like a trial marriage or renting a house before purchase, charter of a boat discloses flaws as well as virtues which assist in making the decision whether to buy. The second reason to charter has nothing to do with ultimate ownership. Sailors in northern waters, who own their boats, may wish to explore the Bahamas or the Caribbean Islands for a winter vacation without facing the huge expense of transporting their own craft. When the scene of exploration is to be the even more distant fjords of Norway or the isles of Greece, chartering a local boat is the only sensible procedure.

An additional reward for chartering comes from the lessons learned from the way other people maintain boats. Sometimes equipment that is quite unknown to the charterer exists aboard a strange boat, and the opportunity to test its usefulness exists without the investment of time and money to try it out on one's own vessel.

At the end of World War II, I knew I wanted to resume sailing, but I had no firm idea of what kind of boat would best serve my rather unsettled purposes. My first free summer, I chartered a 34-foot sloop, for a leisurely two-week cruise around Buzzard's Bay and the adjacent islands. She was a Barnacle Class boat, designed by John Alden in what must have been a moment of aberration. The Barnacle deserved her unpleasant class name; she was ugly, slow, tender, and wet. Quite apart from these miserable qualities and, through no fault of her designer, she had the most dangerous type of stove I've ever encountered. It was fed by gasoline under pressure and, in my opinion, heating food with the fuse of a bomb would have been an equally safe method. The very first day aboard, I sailed to New Bedford and bought a two-burner alcohol stove which I took with me at the end of the charter.

The next two summers offered a welcome contrast to this unpleasant interlude. Both summers, I arranged with a college classmate for a month's charter of his Sparkman and Stephens-designed Weekender sloop. On two cruises to the coast of Maine, I found this thirty-five footer with her high freeboard and wide decks a fast, dry, comfortable sailer even in rough weather. Her major drawback was that she carried an excessive weather helm, so that after a few hours at the tiller in any kind of a breeze, the helmsman's arm felt as if an ingenious medieval torturer had been working on it. Experience gained on these charters determined two requirements for all future boats I might acquire. The first was wheel steering; the second was a yawl rig. The yawl is more adaptable for various wind conditions because, while its small mizzensail furnishes little drive, in strong winds the large mainsail can be left furled while various size jibs in combination with the mizzen furnish adequate speed and easy handling.

During the summers of 1950 and '51 I chartered for thirty-day periods just such a boat as I had envisaged. These vacation cruises on *Skylark* were a successful trial marriage during which both partners were tested thoroughly before forming a permanent union. Explaining why you love a boat is nearly as difficult as explaining why you love a particular woman, although others who do not appeal to you as much may be more beautiful, wittier, and more attractive. Nearly all sailors love their boats with varying intensity or they would not own them, and because of the virtues they discover they forgive the imperfections. The happiest way to introduce yourself to a fellow boat owner is to say: "My, she's a beauty," as you inspect what may be a graceless tub with flaws as noticeable as a wart on a woman's nose. The pleased owner will respond by some such speech as, "She doesn't look like much, but she is very fast in strong winds," or "She's a little heavy but very seaworthy," or "She's fat but she is just what my wife and I need to cruise in with our four children."

So I fell in love with *Skylark* and I love her still although she has passed from my possession. *Skylark* is a 39-foot yawl, built in 1941 of prewar materials, mahogany planking, Sitka spruce spars, an iron keel, and bronze fittings. Because of the war she had not been launched till 1946. The joiner work throughout and particularly the cabinet work in the cabin were a joy to observe. The venerable Major Casey whose yard near New Bedford, Massachusetts, had built her took pride in the superlative skills of his boatwrights. Her lines were graceful, she was a fast sailer in the light winds that prevail during New England's summers, and for these virtues she was forgiven for being wet in a blow, throwing spray back from her finely drawn bow, and burying her deck when sailed close to a strong wind. A gasoline engine drove her during calms at six knots. I bought *Skylark* in 1952 and owned her until 1967, a far longer period than I have ever enjoyed any other vessel.

Two possibilities exist when the purpose of chartering is not prospective ownership but rather exploration of distant waters. The first and more cautious approach is to charter a relatively large vessel which has a captain and crew familiar with the local waters. The more adventurous alternative is the bareboat charter of a small-enough boat to handle oneself with friends as crew. Our first exploration of the beautiful Caribbean islands was on the 65-foot schooner *Bokanier* for a two-week cruise with another couple. *Bokanier* was typical of the crewed charter boats that ply the Virgins, the Greek Islands, and the whole Windward and Leeward chain. The vessel was of ancient vintage, built in England, where she had spent her youth as a private yacht. She had a young Englishman as skipper and two natives of Antigua as deckhand and steward. We boarded the schooner in Martinique and in a fortnight visited St. Lucia, Dominica, Guadeloupe, and Antigua. The trade winds blew steadily at twenty to twenty-five knots which made the passages between the islands rough. A number of the anchorages are not harbors at all but merely roadstands on the lee side of the islands. While they are protected from the wind, the sea swell imparts a slow rolling motion to the boats at anchor. The villages and towns on the islands are of historic interest and considerable natural beauty. We had the good fortune to time our visit with the religious festivities that precede Easter, the time of carnival. The processions, dances, and celebrations of the native population made the visit to these islands memorable.

Most sailboat enthusiasts believe that powerboats are not only the enemy by reason of the wakes they create, but must be noisy bores to navigate, requiring little skill and virtually no seamanship. However, one body of water, certainly among the most scenically splendid in the world, is suited far better for cruising under power than by sail. The inland passage from Seattle to Alaska offers some twelve hundred miles of towering mountains, fjordlike inlets, and plentiful harbors. To explore it, we chartered a fifty-foot motor-boat with an owner who was completely familiar with these waters.

Fog is a threat in the summer months, but in the two weeks of September we were aboard, the fog only once obscured the grandeur of the scene. However, for sailing, the wind is stifled in the narrow channels by the high mountains towering directly from the sea, and the tidal currents are awesome, forming huge whirlpools in places which are favored by the salmon but are lethal for small craft. To see a bear fishing along the shore at dawn, to see the killer whales swimming in their close formation, to watch the salmon jump, and to savor the wonderful oysters, clams, and shrimps which abound are treats that offset the monotonous sound of a powerboat's engine and the tedious routine, at least to sailors, of cruising without sail. Except for the ravages of the lumber companies in British Columbia, this area is unspoiled compared to any portion of our east coast.

Another area which offers great scenic beauty, but little else to the sailor is the Gulf of Baja California, usually known as the Sea of Cortes. I cruised these waters in late December, 1971, for two weeks aboard *Altair III.* She was a motor sailer, that half-breed combination of a powerboat with just enough sail to tantalize the sailor, but not enough to really propel the vessel except in near gales. I had first met the Grays when they were sailing their lovely ketch, *Altair II,* in the Bahamas. It was a "ships that pass in the night" acquaintanceship until chance brought *Shag* and *Altair II* together again in the Virgins over the course of two winters. The Grays, who spend much of each year living aboard whatever vessel they own, had *Altair III* built near Seattle, and her maiden cruise was up the inland passage to Alaska. After that expedition, they sailed and powered *Altair III* down the West Coast of the United States, and I joined them in Le Paz, Mexico, at the tip of the long peninsula of Baja California.

Cruising in Mexico presents several problems, none insurmountable but all decreasing the pleasure of a sailing vacation. In the first place, contrasted with the informality of the Canadians, the Mexicans insist on a virtual blizzard of paperwork to enter or depart from their inhabited ports. I never learned what all the documents were for or even what they meant, but I did learn that the only acceptable method for clearing and entering was to engage a local official for $11 each time to make out all the documents that were required. Secondly, water is in extremely short supply, both to the inhabitants of this arid region, and more par-ticularly to visiting yachtsmen. In the few places it is

138

available it is often not potable. Finally, at least in December and early January, the wind blows hard from the north which makes progress up the gulf a dead tack into head seas. Swimming in the cool water is not a temptation. Despite Steinbeck's handsome description in his *Log of the Sea of Cortes*, it is an area to which I would not return.

By far the most rewarding charter of a crewed vessel that I ever enjoyed was a two weeks' journey among the Galapagos Islands aboard the 88-foot schooner, *Golden Cachalot*. No vessel was ever worse-designed for her mission among the equatorial islands than the fat, slow, poor-sailing, converted Baltic cargo vessel. As the winds in these islands vary between dead calm and extremely gentle, the ventilation on the old North Sea sailer was entirely inadequate. She accommodated ten passengers and was manned by a crew of six Englishmen led by a young captain who could be ideally cast in the lead role of a feature movie about Drake, Raleigh, or the young Mountbatten. *Golden Cachalot* thumped around the accessible islands under powerful diesel engines, as, with all sails set, the wind never had sufficient force to propel her.

The excitement of these islands did not arise from the sailing nor even from the beauty of the sea, although beautiful it is. Porpoises by the hundreds gambol and leap in these waters. The abundant sea lions swim far from the land and laze on the surface with one flipper raised as if to fan themselves. Sea turtles are also abundant and the clouds of birds, some species seen nowhere else in the world, are a continual joy.

The true excitement comes from being present and being able to recreate the birth of one of history's great ideas. Doubtless, nearly everyone has seen an apple

139

fall far from a tree, yet few identify with Newton or his measurements of gravitational force. But Darwin's idea of evolution and the adaptability of the different species to their environment and their need to survive is ever present in the Galapagos. In the first place, there are the many species of finches which obviously all came from a common ancestor, although today, millions of years later, the shapes of their bills to permit feeding on different islands in the chain clearly delineates their differences. Some have long bills to suck honey from cactus, some have hooked bills to crush shells, and some have short straight bills to catch insects. No two of the different species exist together on the same island. Similarly, the thousands of iguanas separate into at least four species. Some of these reptiles swim and catch fish. On another island a similar appearing iguana never goes near the water but lives on vegetation. The ghost of *H.M.S. Beagle* sails in company with all who venture there, and the endless debate which took place more than a century ago between the young naturalist Darwin and the fundamentalist naval officer aboard that vessel is easy to imagine.

The most ideal location I have ever seen for bareboat chartering is the Virgin Islands chain. The waters are deep, the charts are accurate, and navigation is easy. The whole island chain extends only thirty-five miles, and the constantly blowing easterly trade winds guarantee good sailing in nearly all months of the year. The climate is ideal, the swimming and snorkeling in the clear water always inviting and, for those who seek variety ashore, there is a sufficient number of "tourist traps" to satiate the most jaded taste.

My first experience with my own command among the islands was in the winter of 1965 when Jane and I

140

chartered a 30-foot Sea Winds ketch in St. Thomas. This miserable little mass-produced fiberglass boat was both slow and uncomfortable. To make matters worse, the so-called "Christmas winds" decided to arrive in January rather than accompany Santa Claus, and they piped up to velocities between thirty-five and fifty miles an hour during most of our fortnight. Despite the boat's shortcomings, we fell completely in love with the islands. The harbors are snug and close together. It is no punishment to lay over in any of them for a couple of days as your snorkel mask discloses the most dazzling array of tropical fish and magnificent coral formations. The following winter we chartered a 36-foot Alberg sloop which was a vast improvement although the ventilation from her single hatch left something to be desired on hot days or still nights. We sailed in her for two months, exploring every nook and cranny of the island chain and revisiting those that had become our favorites. Provisioning, particularly securing ice and water, presented something of a problem in those years, but it was by no means insurmountable.

Bareboating has proved to be so attractive that over the years the number of agencies offering these boats has multiplied, and the quality of both the boats and the servicing of them has improved immeasurably. For example, on Tortola in the British Virgin Islands at least two American companies operate, both with many desirable, well-kept, and clean boats. Unlike former days, these boats are iced, watered and fueled; and food and wine are put aboard all with no effort on the part of the charterer. For two weeks at the end of 1972, I chartered a 35-foot Pearson sloop from one of these companies and, in the belief that my experience was typical, I can unhesitatingly recommend these efficient bareboat operations. The boat was

141

thoughtfully provisioned with as much variety of food as local conditions permit; it was clean; and every mechanical part that was supposed to work, worked.

Obviously, no charter boat arrangement is as satisfactory as having one's own boat in the waters one wishes to sail. But considering the difficulties and expense of transporting a boat great distances, the charter permits a width of sailing experience available in no other way.

13

Rough Seas and Strong Winds

Sooner or later, everyone who sails will encounter storms. Even day sailors who return to their home harbor each evening will experience a summer thundersquall. For those who venture offshore, these unwelcome interludes are inevitable. The fury of any particular storm is a subjective assessment. Tacking into a twenty-knot wind can be a nightmare if you are aboard a 15-foot boat; aboard a 40-foot cruiser, it is a delightful sailing breeze. However, there are meteorological disturbances that, regardless of the size of the vessel, all observers agree pose a distinct threat to all who are at sea at the time.

143

My first experience with such a storm occurred on the Fourth of July of my third year of sailing at Marblehead, in *Rose II*. The severity of Marblehead's thundersqualls are noteworthy along the whole New England Coast. Meteorologists explain that due to the funnel shape of neighboring Salem Harbor, these occasional storms are concentrated so that their winds are far fiercer than those experienced in neighboring areas. During these storms, branches break off, electrical wires are severed and boats not securely moored are swept across the harbor. These storms give little advance notice of their arrival, and there seems to be no way that the "busters" can be differentiated ahead of time from the harmless summer squalls which bring heavy downpours of rain but little wind.

Independence Day is an occasion for a major regatta wherever sailboats race, and Marblehead is no exception. July 4, 1928, was a sparkling summer day, and every boat in the fleet answered her starter's gun that afternoon. White sails spread for miles across the placid sea. An hour after the Triangles started, black storm clouds gathered behind Salem Harbor. We had no doubt the squall would advance towards us, but we hoped it would hold off long enough to permit us to finish the course. For once, we were well up in the fleet in perhaps fifth or sixth position as we rounded the last mark and headed for the finish line, a scant three miles away. It soon became obvious that we were not going to reach shelter in time. A wind-driven white wall of hail and rain swept toward us.

"Get the sails down," I ordered.

The crew member whose duty it was to watch our competitors and judge our relative position reported, "The leaders aren't taking their sails down."

"I don't care," I said. "We are. It's just a race."

The author taking Shag *to windward in 1972.*

We were barely in time. The squall hit us just as the last ties were thrown over the furled sails. Never before had we seen any storm that approached the ferocity of that wind. Hail blinded us, rain streamed down in torrents, and the wind reached a high screaming note. I turned *Rose II*'s stern to the wind's fury and we ran under the bare mast away from the finish line. We could not see any other boats; indeed, we could not see the bow of our own. We felt as though we were on a "Nantucket sleigh ride," on a small boat, attached by the harpoon line to a whale. It was over within twenty minutes. Drenched by the downpour, teeth chattering with cold, we reset our sails and headed for the finish line.

With the return of visibility, we could see that Massachusetts Bay was a disaster area. Several boats which had tried to sail through the squall were dismasted, their crews trying to clear the tangled rigging and torn sails as we passed by. Powerboats were scurrying around pulling the crews of capsized craft from the water. We sailed past the upside-down hull of one large motorboat which had left the harbor with all her canvas awnings firmly secured in place. As we crossed the finish line, we saw the members of the regatta committee, usually relaxed and seated with cold drinks in their hands, anxiously taking count of the surviving boats.

The storm was front page news the next day. Three of the occupants of the capsized motorboat had drowned, trapped in the cabin where they had retreated from the storm. Nine of the little O boats had capsized, and to everyone's amazement had sunk. Fortunately the yacht club launches on rescue duty picked up all of the swimming sailors. There were too many dismastings for a full count, but several people had received minor injuries from falling spars. The Coast Guard reported that the wind had reached a velocity of seventy miles an hour as the storm crossed Salem Harbor.

In the open ocean, a wind of that strength would have created huge waves but, under the lee of the Massachusetts Coast, there was insufficient room for the seas to build. There exist places where the seas can be horrendous even without strong winds. The first year that we owned my staunch 40-foot yawl, *Shag,* we planned a winter in the Bahamas. The run from Miami to the nearest island is only around sixty miles, but in the short daylight periods of winter, part of the voyage has to be made at night.

In the afternoon of December 15, 1967, we left our dock at Miami for the passage across the Gulf Stream to Gun Cay in the Bahamas. The wind in Biscayne Bay was light, and *Shag* glided toward the ocean with all sail set. Once we left the bay, conditions changed rapidly. The wind freshened from the north, creating a confused sea in opposition to the flow of the north-bound Gulf Stream current. I furled the mainsail, and *Shag* plowed into the mounting waves under small jib and mizzen. Seas swept the decks, spray shot up to the height of the spreaders and drenched us; even the cockpit stayed half full of water despite its self-bailing feature. Curiously enough, the waves came aboard the boat from the lee side as well as from the direction of the wind. In addition, the crests of waves came in over the stern. There was no rhythm to the confused and extremely rough sea. Jane went below for the safety harness and oilskins and emerged pale from the cabin.

"I still can say I've never been seasick but only just. Did you know it was going to be like this?"

"I've never been here before in my life," I told her

147

as a defense for the discomfort I was inflicting. For five hours we endured the punishment of wild motion combined with soaking spray. Finally, around midnight we sighted the white light on Gun Cay flashing every ten seconds. It took us three more hours before I dropped the anchor in the placid waters of the little island's lee.

"You can get yourself a new mate if you intend to do that very often," Jane told me.

I made some inane remark about the boat behaving well under difficult conditions, but it was the scrambled eggs and coffee laced with whiskey that transformed incipient mutiny into reluctant acceptance. When we lay down to sleep on the soaked berths, Jane murmured something to the effect that everyone who wanted to cruise the Bahamas had to cross the Gulf Stream and maybe it had not been all that bad.

Since that night, I have crossed the Stream three times, and it was never that bad again. But under any conditions, the Stream is an awesome body of water.

There are other places that, either because of the geologic formation or strong tidal currents, seem always to have extremely rough seas regardless of the force of the wind. Cape Sable is one of them. The tides in the Bay of Fundy are world famous for their enormous rise and fall, and, as trillions of gallons of water flow into the Atlantic past Cape Sable, huge waves and very severe tide rips result. My first venture to the Nova Scotia coast was with an all-male crew in *Skylark*. Mike had sailed with me since the earliest days and was a regular crew member when his work schedule permitted. The facet of small boat life that particularly aroused Mike's pride of performance was cooking. He fancied himself as one of the great sea cooks of his era and perhaps of any era. As a matter of fact, he was pretty good. On the second night after leaving Marblehead, we approached the tide-plagued waters near Cape Sable. As dawn approached, we were running in fog and Fundy's tides were meeting the Atlantic swells, so that *Skylark* was performing gyrations that made footing unsteady and stomachs queasy. I made some idle remark that I could now understand why sailors in the Bermuda Race were forced to diet on sandwiches or dry shredded wheat.

"Crap," announced Mike. "Anyone who can't prepare a hot meal at any time at sea isn't entitled to call himself a 'seacook'". I suggested mildly that if he sincerely felt that way, scrambled eggs, bacon, and coffee would be welcome.

Mike accepted the challenge. He lit the stove, clamped on pot holders, braced himself between stove and icebox and succeeded in preparing breakfast. Nearly succeeded I should say. Just as he removed the pot clamps to serve the food, a swell that had been born weeks before off the coast of Spain met the maximum ebb tide of Fundy's fabulous current. Eggs flew in one direction, bacon in another, coffee in still another. Even though our tongues were watering, those of us on deck laughed till we cried. Not so Mike. Piece by piece, he picked up the bacon, the only solid thing that he could still grab, and hurled it at the nonoffending stove, cursing the while with a variety and volume that would have done credit to his earlier Army career as a military policeman.

I have been around Cape Sable five times since that initial experience, and only once was the sea relatively smooth. On my last crossing, a new feature was added. In *Shag* we left Shelburne bound for Marblehead in fair weather with a southeast wind behind us. The weather reports forecast a gale well off Cape Cod and no threat to the mainland. As we passed Cape Sable, which we for once were able to see as there was no fog, the wind increased so we took in our spinnaker. The sea around the cape was relatively quiet, perhaps at slack tide. As the day wore on, the wind increased to perhaps twenty-five knots, fog and rain accompanied the rising velocity. We furled the mainsail and proceeded comfortably on our course under a small jib and the mizzen. About fifty miles past the cape, the seas became confused and extremely rough. As in the Gulf Stream, there was no rhythm to the waves and they struck the boat from every direction.

"What in the world is this all about?" one of my crew asked.

I studied the chart, making a small cross at our estimated position.

"Well, whatever it may mean, according to the chart we are in the center of the Truxton Swell. There seems to be a bank here where the sea shoals to only three hundred or four hundred feet."

Even this far from Cape Sable, Fundy's tides work their mischief over this uneven contour of the sea bottom.

If a yachtsman, sailing port-to-port in daytime along the coast, is forewarned by weather reports of an approaching gale, he seeks the nearest snug harbor, lowers his heaviest anchor with plenty of scope, and awaits the inclement weather. However, sometimes gale force winds arrive completely unheralded. In our initial cruise to the Bahamas in newly commissioned *Shag,* we experienced one of these unannounced "busters."

For a month, we had visited various of the sandy little cays that characterize the southern part of the Bahamas chain. Usually, we only stayed overnight in the same place unless we particularly liked the spot. One of our longest layovers was in the snug little harbor at the southernmost tip of Abaco. The only inhabitants of this lovely but isolated spot were the lighthouse keeper and his family and an American sculptor who had built a home there. A memorable experience resulted from meeting the lighthouse keeper's wife. She had raised a wild boar from infancy which her young son had found abandoned and help-less. The pig was two years-old when we were there and was as tame as the two huge dogs that were the other family pets. The pig, with no other animal companionship, seemed to think itself a dog. It fol-lowed the family on its ramblings to the beach where it went swimming with the dogs and the humans. We were sad to leave this charming place and had cause to be even sadder the night after we left its perfectly protected anchorage.

We sailed a short way to the north and anchored off a tiny village that clustered around an industrial salt operation. The land offered perfect protection from the south and west, the direction from which the wind was blowing on our arrival. But just before sunset a blustering "norther," completely unheralded by either the Miami or Nassau Weather Bureau, swept across the anchorage. There was nothing gentle about its arrival. The wind reversed and almost immediately was blowing between fifty and sixty knots. Our 20-pound Danforth anchor, which had been adequate for the soft wind that had prevailed, pulled out on the wind reversal, and we dragged nearly to the threatening land that had originally been our protection. The diesel engine, running at full speed, was barely able to inch us ahead into the teeth of the howling wind.

With Jane at the wheel, I struggled to get out the big

151

50-pound yachtsman's anchor that lay under all the sails in the sail locker. It had never been used, and I had not had the foresight to cut the wires that had been used to hold the parts together for shipment. It took me what seemed hours to get wire cutters, attach a new shackle, and finally rig the big unwieldy anchor to a spare anchor line. In reality, it took no more than fifteen minutes, but that was long enough to allow the wind to whip the sea into an angry froth of short, steep waves. *Shag* plunged like a tortured horse with her bow plunging under the swiftly passing crests.

Jane had managed to claw about two hundred yards away from the threatening lee shore by the time I was ready with the big anchor. Merely by throttling down the engine, *Shag* lost her headway in the face of that gale, and I first lowered a 35-pound Danforth and let out around a hundred feet of scope. I then lowered the big yachtsman anchor and allowed *Shag* to fall back another hundred feet until we were nearly at the end of the Danforth's line. We did not take *Shag*'s motor out of gear until we could plainly hear the groans from the heavy nylon anchor lines signifying that both anchors had taken firm hold. By this time it was dark, and we carefully took bearings on lights ashore so that we could detect dragging if it occurred. But, in truth, had we dragged there was nothing we could have done except allow *Shag* to drift to the beach and try somehow to get ashore from her wreckage. The anchors held.

All night long we were watchfully awake. The nearest protection from the north was at least three miles away; we might as well have been anchored in the open Atlantic. Every few seconds, *Shag*'s bow would plunge into an oncoming wave, and throw back spray like a dog shaking itself. The noise of the spray hitting the canvas dodger we rigged sounded like machine gun fire. At hour intervals, I went forward to let out a few more feet on each anchor line and replace the chafing gear that I had affixed to protect the rope.

Despite my precautions, the force of the gale unravelled both nylon ropes so that new ones had to be purchased when we returned to the States. The night seemed endless, nor did conditions improve at daybreak. The distress frequency on the radio chronicled marine disasters all along the island chain as a result of the unannounced arrival of the "norther." By the second night we were exhausted, but becoming accustomed to *Shag*'s wild gyrations. We took turns sleeping and keeping an anchor watch. By the next morning, the worst was over. Boats put out from the shore to inquire about our welfare, but by then all we wanted was sleep. The whole experience did little to enhance our enthusiasm for Bahama's cruising.

Anyone who lives on the eastern seaboard of the United States, as I do, has had at least one encounter with a hurricane. I have had many. Sometimes several summers can pass without a visit from one of these rampaging ladies; during other summers two or even three of these violent storms will hit the New England coast. Safely ensconced in a well-built house, you can survey the carnage from a window while thanking God that you are not out in a small boat. A relatively low building in midtown Manhattan is a poor vantage point for observing weather conditions so, while September 21, 1938, seemed a miserable, rainy, windy afternoon as I looked out my office window, I had no idea that a devastating hurricane was passing through the city. The accounts of the destruction in the next morning's newspapers surprised me, but it was not until I reached my office that the storm directly touched my life.

The switchboard operator called me almost as soon as I was seated at my desk and told me that the president of the Western Union Telegraph Company wanted to talk to me. Somewhat surprised at a call from such a high official of a company with which I had had no contact, I picked up the phone.

The voice asked, "Are you the owner of a sailboat about forty feet long named *Rose?*"

I admitted it.

"Well, it's in the middle of my lawn."

"How in the world did it get there?" I asked, somewhat stunned by this bizarre information.

"The storm washed it up there yesterday afternoon, but the water was so high, I couldn't identify it until this morning," he told me.

"I'm awfully sorry," I assured him. "I'll try to get it out of your way as soon as possible."

"It's not your fault," he said, "and it's not particularly in my way. It's just odd to have a sailboat on your lawn."

I asked him where he lived and he gave me an address in Oyster Bay.

Oyster Bay is about nine miles down Long Island Sound from Rye as well as six miles across. I had left *Rose* safely moored in Rye only a couple of days before, and my imagination played on what the condition of my beautiful boat must be after grounding at the end of a pilotless voyage of such length in a full hurricane. Nor was my apprehension lessened as I drove along the north shore road of Long Island. The destruction was almost unbelievable. Port Washington, the first harbor I had an opportunity to observe, was a tangle of wrecked boats, piled in intertwining chaos on the shore. Once-proud schooners, with large holes in their sides and their masts broken and hanging by their

154

rigging, were lying on top of splintered motorboats. It seemed that a hundred vessels were mixed in this burial pile.

The sights along the road bore further evidence of the storm's fury. Huge trees lay in a tangle of branches with their roots exposed. A rowboat hung with its bow jammed into the second-story window of one beach house. Obviously it had been caught there when someone tried to rescue the occupants of the house. It was very nearly impossible to envisage the sea which now lay placidly several hundred yards from this house reaching the level of a second-story window.

When I drove down the lane of the Oyster Bay address I had been given, I could see *Rose*'s mast tilted at a 45 degree angle. There lay the boat in the middle of a well-kept lawn which gradually sloped to a sand beach bordering the sea. The vessel was about thirty yards from the water and perhaps ten feet above the present placid water level. As the boat had a draft of six feet, the level of the sea that had deposited it in its present recumbent position must have been at least sixteen feet above normal levels. Imagination refused to accept the force of a storm that would raise Long Island Sound to such a catastrophic level.

As I approached the stranded boat I could not see any broken planks or the marks of damage which had been the universal characteristic of Port Washington's wreckage. As I walked around the boat examining it closely, I could see no scars whatever, not even scratches in the paint. I climbed on the sharply tilted hull and unlocked the cabin hatch. Preliminary inspection disclosed nothing amiss. I climbed down into the cabin to find the drinking glasses unbroken in their rack, the ash tray still sitting between the low rails of the table; indeed nothing was out of its normal place.

155

Incredibly, *Rose* had sawn through her mooring rope, drifted over Scotch Caps, the line of rocks that border Rye Harbor, sailed before the gale some nine miles, beached herself, and remained absolutely unscathed throughout her ordeal.

From the house I telephoned a boatyard on City Island and explained *Rose*'s plight. In a few hours a small tug boat approached the beach and anchored as closely as the depth permitted. A rowboat brought ashore two men with several lengths of steel pipe and the end of a heavy hawser from the tug. The tide was nearly high when the pipes were placed in a path which *Rose* could roll over toward the beach. The hawser was attached to the heavy bitt on *Rose*'s bow, and the tug's powerful winch took up the slack in the line. Just before high tide the winch began to turn and *Rose*, aided by the gradual seaward slope of the lawn, began her bumpy journey over the steel pipes to the sea. She reached the sandy beach at the exact moment of high tide. Within a few minutes, the straining hawser had pulled her into deep water where she floated proudly, still completely undamaged after her miraculous escape from destruction. The tugboat towed her to an early winter storage on City Island, her only punishment in the great hurricane of 1938.

Since 1938, the weather bureau has improved its forecasting of the arrival of these devastating storms. Airplanes track them from their birth in the Caribbean and follow their paths to their deaths on the land or over the cold waters of the North Atlantic. Repeated warnings of their approach furnish adequate time for the cruising yachtsman to seek safe refuge. I have been safely at anchor in two of them. The first was the tail end of an August hurricane in Nova Scotia. We found refuge in good time in a lovely landlocked cove in the

Bras d'Or Lakes on Cape Breton Island. The high spruce trees that surrounded the cove reduced the wind force to no more than a breeze, but the rain was almost not to be believed. The Halifax Weather Bureau reported an eight and a half inch rainfall in four hours. Except in New Guinea and the Solomon Islands during the war, I have never seen rain like that. In the first two hours of the storm, "Judas" filled with water and sank. The line to the stern allowed us to retrieve him when the storm passed.

The second hurricane that occurred was Abby, that errant storm which circled endlessly over Pennsylvania and New England causing severe floods and millions of dollars of damage. Moored to a dock in perfectly protected Northeast Harbor, Maine, *Shag* was in no danger whatever. After the third day of rain and gale force winds, we deserted the vessel and repaired to an adjacent motel until the storm ended.

Just once, I was not so lucky. The fourth hurricane of the summer of 1954, like its sisters since time immemorial, had been spawned in the eastern reaches of the Caribbean. The Miami Weather Bureau had picked it up, almost at its birth, and Navy patrol planes reported its daily progress as it wended its slow, random course first to the west and then to the north. It brushed past some of the Caribbean islands, dropping tons of rain, but, while it was a full-fledged hurricane with winds of eighty miles an hour, it was not a killer storm of the gravest proportions. Nonetheless, a hurricane is to be feared whenever it nears a land mass, and the residents of Florida, who have had more experience with these disturbances than inhabitants of most parts of the eastern seaboard, are particularly sensitive to the threat. The Miami Weather Bureau posted a hurricane watch for Florida's Atlantic coast, but cancelled it when the storm veered to a more northerly course before even reaching the Bahamas. The North Carolina Capes were the next potential danger area, and the weather bureau warned the area to prepare to receive the unwelcome visitor. But again, the storm altered its erratic course away from the land. The Virginia coast was the final land mass to receive the weather bureau's "Alert," but again the storm obligingly veered away.

I had, of course, followed the hurricane's progress by both radio report and the weather maps published in newspapers, so I was gratified on the beautiful sunny August Saturday to hear the weather bureau's announcement that the hurricane no longer posed a threat to any part of the American continent. In view of the favorable forecast, we commenced our plan for a normal weekend run in *Skylark* down to Port Jefferson on Saturday, to return to Mamaroneck the following day. *Skylark* had made this untaxing voyage so many times that she had figuratively worn tracks in Long Island Sound. On this weekend my crew consisted of Helen, the wife of a good friend whose passion for tennis rivalled his wife's love of sailing, so that after some thirty years of marriage each frequently went their separate recreational ways. The other crew member was Ralph, the navigator of *U.S.S. Gen. John Pope* during the last year I was aboard that vessel, and in 1954 a construction supervisor for a large building contractor. Ralph had been to sea as a merchant seaman for years, and after his discharge from the Navy had been a navigator on Pan American's transatlantic flights until the airlines decided to assign navigational duties to copilots.

The run to Port Jefferson was pleasant and uneventful, with a soft following wind which permitted us to set our spinnaker. The thirty-seven miles were covered in five hours, so we had time to anchor in the protected harbor for a swim. The evening weather forecast over the radio predicted sunny skies and soft southerly winds for the morrow, and the next morning fulfilled the predictions. After a leisurely breakfast, we sailed from Port Jefferson in a moderate southeasterly wind for the run back to Mamaroneck.

Some thirteen miles west of Port Jefferson is Eatons Point, which boasts one of the most powerful lighthouses on the whole coast, plus a large Coast Guard station which commands a sweeping view of the Sound. As we approached the point around noon, I noticed two flags flying under the stars and stripes on the Coast Guard's flagpole.

"What's the Coast Guard got flying, Ralph?" I asked.

He picked up a pair of binoculars and studied the flagpole. "They got the hurricane signal flying," he said. "Two red flags with black centers on top of each other."

"Wouldn't you think the Coast Guard would listen to the radio once in a while?" I said. "Those flags ought to have been pulled down yesterday."

"I didn't notice them when we passed yesterday," he said. "But you know the story of the treaty between the rabbits and the foxes."

"No," I said, playing the straight man, "What's the story about the rabbits and the foxes?"

"Well," he said warming up to his joke, "the leaders of the rabbits made a peace treaty with the chief of the foxes. All the rabbits and the foxes sat around a campfire passing a peace pipe along. All of a sudden, one frightened bunny comes dashing out of the woods across the campground with a fox in pursuit. 'Hey rabbit,' his leader yelled after him, 'you don't have to run. We've made a peace treaty with the foxes.' The fleeing bunny, without slackening his speed, yelled back at the rabbit leader, 'Maybe so, but there's always some sleepy son of a bitch that doesn't get the word.'"

Then we saw it. Sweeping toward us from the deep indentation of Huntington Bay was a white wall, a seething barrier of wind-driven rain approaching us with the speed of an express train. I started the engine as I yelled, "We got to get the sails down. Helen, if you love us, keep this thing headed into the wind or we'll be overboard."

Skylark's bow headed into the approaching wall with Helen at the wheel, while Ralph and I hurried to the mast. Usually in times of crisis Murphy's law operates—"Anything that can go wrong, will"—but on this day the sails came sliding down with no snarled coils or other hindrance. By the time the storm reached us, we had the jib furled and lashed, the mainsail furled and we were engaged in tying lashings around it. The wind blew the big sail free and it became an unmanageable, flogging mass of cloth. Using all of our strength to tame the billowing sail, Ralph and I struggled to get ties around it.

From the wheel, Helen yelled, "I've lost steerage way. I can't hold her in the wind." The engine which was powerful enough to drive the boat at six knots in calm water was helpless in the face of the roaring wind. Indeed, the boat was being driven backward although the engine was turning at full speed ahead. We managed to get three ties around the unruly mainsail by the time the boat turned from the wind's eye to broadside. She was knocked right over on her side by the force of the wind even though all sails were down. Water surged knee-deep up on her decks. I clawed my way back to the wheel and turned the boat so that we ran before the hurricane. Visibility was absolutely zero. The rain was so torrential, augmented by wind-driven spray, that it was impossible to see even ten feet. Under the bare masts, with nothing but the hull resisting the wind's force, *Skylark* began going so fast that her bow lifted and she dragged her stern in the water. Strangely enough, the sea was relatively smooth. The wind was so strong that it blew the tops off of the short steep waves which had only a limited opportunity to build because of the lee formed by Long Island's landmass. With relatively little rocking motion, *Skylark* plunged forward at more than her designed maximum speed.

Of course, we were soaked. There had been no chance to don oilskins, and we were shivering. No one thought then or later to get out the life preservers and put them on although, in retrospect, it would have been a sensible thing to do. We just crouched in the cockpit hanging on to whatever part of the boat was near our hands and tried to look ahead. I had never been in a small boat with a wind force comparable to that. The violent blasts of thundersqualls around Marblehead where wind speeds reached sixty-five or seventy knots (which I had experienced years earlier) seemed almost gentle compared to this howling tempest. It was impossible to stand upright and equally impossible to face astern and look into the wind. The pain of the lashing rain on bare skin was beyond bearing.

The wind was from a little south of east, so that we were running before it on a course a little north of due west. From Eatons Point to the narrow entrance of the East River is only about fifteen miles.

"We haven't a hell of a lot of sea room," I yelled. "If

this lasts more than a couple of hours, we're going to be blown ashore."

"We ought to try to slow her down," Ralph yelled.

"Yeah. How do you do that?" I asked.

"Drag ropes," he said.

We did the best we could. We tied every available loose line in the cockpit to cleats and threw the bights overboard to trail astern. It had no appreciable effect on the boat's speed.

"That's a pretty funny story you've got about not getting the word," I yelled at Ralph.

Just then a barely discernible shape crossed just ahead of our bow. Another boat in the same plight but on a slightly different course had missed us by only a few feet.

"That's all we need," Ralph yelled, "to get hit by another boat."

The danger was real. This was a Sunday in August with the traffic on Long Island Sound at its peak, and the storm completely unexpected. Many other boats, blindly rushing at maximum speed, had to be near us.

Our blind progress at full speed continued for more than two hours. We had no choice as to our course; we had to run before the wind-driven torrent of rain and spray. From time to time we would catch a glimpse of a fleeing shadow on a parallel course as we came within yards of other boats in the same predicament. As in other dreadful human dilemmas, time made us almost accustomed to our uncomfortable and dangerous progress. We talked, or rather yelled at each other, above the roar of the wind about how much time we had left before we piled up on some unknown rocks at the western end of the sound. Even though we had no accurate knowledge of our position, we knew that our sea room was becoming painfully short.

Then as suddenly as it had come, the storm stopped. Within a matter of minutes, the wind dropped to a virtual calm, the torrential rain abruptly ceased, and a pale sun made its appearance above us.

"It's the eye," said Ralph. "The hurricane isn't over. Within a short time the wind will come from the opposite direction."

"At least we'll be able to tell where we are," I said as the visibility lengthened behind the retreating rain.

We all looked for familiar landmarks and to our delight found that, while our course had taken us down the center of the sound, we were directly off Mamaroneck Harbor.

"How long do you think the eye will last?" I asked Ralph.

"A half an hour. Not much more," he guessed. "It's a small hurricane or we wouldn't have gotten out of that side of it so soon."

"Well, half an hour is enough," I said. "We're less than two miles from the harbor."

With the engine running at full speed, we entered the familiar opening of our home harbor and picked up our mooring under the shelter of the land. Within minutes the rain started again, and no doubt on the open sound the wind resumed its awesome force. At our mooring, the blasts were diverted by the land as the wind came in from the northwest on the other side of the retreating hurricane's eye. We retreated down into the soaked cabin to look for dry clothes, but nothing remained dry. The wind-driven rain had drenched everything as thoroughly as if buckets of water had been emptied there. Within a couple of hours, the

163

hurricane had passed. Still soaking wet, we walked to a diner and ordered hamburgers and coffee.

"Not much of a day to sail," the counterman said as he put the food down in front of us.

"No," I agreed. "It was blowing pretty good out there."

14

Help When Help Is Needed

The oldest tradition of the sea dictates that all who are
in a position to help the distressed mariner must offer
assistance. Fortunately, it is an extremely rare occurrence when one yachtsman actually requires the assistance of others in order to survive. Well-equipped
boats have radio telephones, and the Coast Guard
maintains a complex air-sea rescue service which re-
sponds to calls over the distress frequency. Distress is
relative. The crew of a sailboat without an engine
becalmed far from a harbor may feel distress that they
will be late getting ashore, but they are in no danger.
In gale weather along the coast, there are so few
vessels venturing forth that one in trouble is not apt to
see others and, even if he did, little in the way of
assistance could be offered.

The most frequent requests for assistance in coastal sailing come from boats lost in fog. In *Skylark* Jane and I had left snug little Sachem's Head in fair weather. We had intended to go as far as the Connecticut River but, soon after our departure, the fog came in, reducing visibility to a few hundred feet. Jane hated and feared the fog as a result of her dreadful experience in the *Andrea Doria,* so I assured her we would cut short our run and anchor in the harbor of refuge at Duck Island. I set a course for the big bell buoy off the Clinton breakwater, which is only about a half mile from Duck Island. When we had run the amount of time I estimated was necessary to be near the bell, we turned off our engine to listen for its chime. We did not hear it, but we did hear a boat's foghorn fairly close at hand. I turned the motor back on and proceeded another quarter of a mile. This time the foghorn was closer, and each time the other vessel blew we responded. Jane, fearing being involved in another collision, was near hysteria. This time I also heard the bell buoy we were aiming for. We proceeded toward it until we saw it and set a new course for Duck Island. The other boat's foghorn was now very near. Suddenly, we saw the other sloop very near us. The skipper was waving and shouting, and I again stopped the engine.

"We've had a hell of a time catching up to you,"he told me. "We're lost. Do you know where we are?" I told him that we were within a few hundred yards of the Clinton breakwater and gave him the course we were steering for Duck Island. He thanked me and followed us to the harbor.

I said to Jane, "If that silly man had just turned off his engine and listened, he would have found the buoy."

Jane said, "He's disgusting. You know he had children on that boat, and he didn't know what he was doing."

I did not argue, but I had been similarly lost too many times to be all that censorious.

After we were anchored under the protection of the island, we went ashore to stretch our legs. We walked out along the huge stones on the breakwater. Faintly from seaward we heard shouts of "Help, help!" I yelled back, but the only response was repeated cries for help.

"We'll have to go back out," I told Jane. We returned to *Skylark*, raised her anchor and crept out of the fog-enshrouded harbor. I turned her bow toward where I believed the cries had come from and listened. We were getting closer. A few hundred yards further, we came on two boys about ten or twelve years old in an outboard motorboat. They were tied to a buoy that marked the island's shoal. They were cold and they were scared.

"What's your problem?" I asked as I came alongside.

"We're lost and we ran out of gas trying to find land," the older boy told me.

I threw them a line and towed their boat back to the anchorage. They came aboard when we were safely back under the island's lee. Jane made them some hot food while I elicited their parents' telephone number. On the ship-to-shore phone, I reached the very frightened parents of these overdue children. Eventually, a boat from the shore sent by the parents took them back to their homes.

"I have a lot more sympathy for those kids than I do for that adult idiot that was lost out there," Jane told me.

So did I.

The white dome that houses *Shag*'s radar antenna and is attached to her mizzenmast notifies other boats that we possess electronic vision that penetrates fog. As a result, other boats ask us to let them follow us when visibility shuts down. They are not in distress in any sense but, in most cases, they would choose to remain at anchor rather than grope around blindly in the fog. The radar has transformed *Shag* into a kind of Seeing Eye guide dog. There have been many instances of our assuming this role, but one is memorable.

The coast of Maine had been enshrouded with fog for a week as a result of one of the typical New England heat waves. During that period we had proceeded along the coast without difficulty, staying up the bays where the fog is always less thick than at sea. Our eventual destination was the St. John River in New Brunswick, but it was a leisurely port-to-port cruise as we were in no hurry. The fog always gets worse as you venture east of Schoodic Point where you can say the Bay of Fundy really begins. We left Northeast Harbor with a fine wind and visibility of perhaps a mile. The fog thickened as we crossed the bottom of Frenchman Bay, and at Schoodic Point the visibility was zero. With the radar, we stayed exactly one-half mile off the coast as we ran up to Prospect Harbor, a small fishing village and the first easily accessible harbor after rounding Schoodic. There was only one yacht at anchor among the fishing boats, and when we waved our greeting after anchoring we could see that only one person was aboard. On our way ashore in "Judas" we stopped alongside the little sloop, and her skipper asked in a disgusted voice, "Is this damn fog ever going to lift?" I laughed and made

168

some remark about its being a beautiful coast if you could ever see it.

"I've been here eight days," he told us. "I won't sail in fog."

"Good heavens," I replied, "Where are you trying to get to?"

"Cutler," he told us. "My wife is going nuts because it is only one day's sail from here, and she's sick of being alone. So am I. I figured it would only take a couple of days from Boothbay, but I'm stuck here."

"We're going to Cape Split tomorrow. If you want to follow us, you're welcome to."

"Oh, I don't know," he hesitated. "If you lost me out there, I'd be in a hell of a shape."

"I won't lose you," I promised. "You may lose sight of me, but there is no way the radar will lose sight of you."

The next morning was flat calm, and the fog was as thick as ever. As we prepared to depart, our new companion yelled over, "I'll go with you, but I can only make five knots in this boat."

"It's all right," I replied. "This boat has a throttle. We'll accommodate to your speed."

It was clear from his voice that he was extremely nervous about this venture, and he became even more anxious as the two boats were occasionally invisible to each other even though they were never more than two hundred feet apart. We set a course for the lighthouse on Petit Manan Island, and when we rounded that outpost offshore, he seemed to gain confidence in our navigational skills. Actually, the whole trip was without incident as our electronic eye picked up the islands and buoys without difficulty. Anchored in Cape Split harbor, he yelled across pointing to the radar dome, "That damn thing is a miracle."

169

"It is, indeed," I agreed.

These incidents were more in the nature of a favor done than an actual assist to someone in dire straits. The one real rescue in which I was involved did not originate in a distress call and I failed, at least partially, in my effort. In June of 1939, one beautiful Sunday afternoon, Jacquette, Charlie, my faithful crew since boyhood, and I were out for a relaxed day sail in my 38-foot cutter, *Rose*. It was as unlikely a setting for a fatal tragedy as could be imagined. In the morning we had drifted from our anchorage in Rye to Oyster Bay in a very light easterly wind. Around one o'clock, as the land mass warmed up in the summer sun and created the typical radiation effect of the hot air rising, a fresh southwest wind came in from the Long Island shore. After eating some sandwiches, we close-hauled our sails and turned around for the reach back to Rye.

It was blowing between fifteen and eighteen knots as we headed for home. This was just a fine sailing breeze for *Rose,* and we kept up all the sails we had set in the morning. The racing fleet was engaged in its usual Sunday contest from Larchmont and, as we caught up with the smaller classes, we noticed they were having a rough, wet sail in their light boats. Crews were hiking out as far as they could on the windward rails to counterbalance the force of the wind as they tacked for the finish line.

The internationally famous Star boats composed the nearest class to us. These classic little keel sloops are built to the same design all over the world, so that racing them in such events as the Olympic games tests the ability of skippers and crews rather than the ingenuity of naval architects. The leading boats in the race were at some distance from us, but it became clear that our course would intercept the class tailenders.

170

The obligation of a skipper just out for a day sail is to avoid interfering in any way with racing boats either by taking wind from their sails or obstructing their course. Therefore, we changed our direction to bring us further astern of the racers.

A puff of wind hit the Star nearest us, and to our amazement the little vessel at first heeled sharply, then toppled over. Small centerboard boats can capsize but keel boats cannot. The weight of the keel prevents their turning upside-down. However, if a keel boat fills with water, either as a result of heeling so far that the sea fills the cockpit over the side or a wave overcomes the boat from astern, it will eventually sink. We were perhaps a quarter of a mile from the little boat when it went over on its side and failed to return to an upright position.

"I guess we better go over and see if they need help," I said.

Charlie agreed and asked, "Why in the world do you suppose they didn't let go the mainsheet or at least luff into the wind?" Either of these maneuvers would have reduced the force of the wind puff on their boat to a harmless rattling of the sails.

"I don't know, Charlie. Maybe they're just learning to sail. Tell you what we'll do, I'll sail to just below them and then head into the wind. When we come up, you lower all the sails and I'll start the engine. She will be easier to handle without all this canvas up."

We felt no great compulsion for haste in carrying out our plan. Within five or six minutes we would be alongside the little vessel which was still floating on its side as a result of air trapped in the hull. The sea was not rough, the June water temperature permitted comfortable swimming, and floating in it for a long period would present no problem to anyone young enough to race the tender little Star boats, particularly when they could hold on to the floating hull.

We sailed to within about fifty yards of the overturned boat, I put the wheel down, and *Rose* faced into the wind with all her sails ashiver. Charlie went to the mast, threw the halyards off their cleats and all three sails tumbled down on deck. I had a little difficulty starting the engine. I choked it too much and it took a minute or two before *Rose* was forging ahead into the wind's eye.

As we came alongside the floating boat, we saw a man holding on to part of the rigging. We threw him a rope and Charlie and I pulled him aboard *Rose*. He was a terribly shaken young man, pale and gasping for breath.

"Where's Eric?" he panted. "Where's Eric?"

"Who's Eric?" I asked.

"Eric is the skipper. I lost sight of him. Where's Eric?"

He was shivering now, and emotionally near the breaking point.

"Jackie," I ordered, "take him below and give him a towel and a great big drink of whisky."

Charlie and I looked at each other for a few seconds as we recognized for the first time the seriousness of the situation.

"You'd better dive in and look for him, Charlie," I said. "He may be trapped under the sail or somewhere."

Charlie stripped to his underwear and dove overboard. He swam under the little boat's hull and emerged on the other side shaking his head.

"Stay the hell away from it, Charlie," I yelled. "It's going to sink."

As he swam clear, the little vessel, having exhausted

the air reservoir that had provided its buoyancy, sank and disappeared from our view. Charlie swam around for perhaps ten minutes, peering from time to time into the depths before I yelled, "Come aboard, Charlie, we can search for him better in the boat."

By the time Charlie was aboard, Jackie and the young man, who told us his name was Bill, were back in the cockpit.

"What happened?" I asked him.

"We were having sandwiches so we tied the mainsheet. I don't know why Eric didn't release the tiller when the puff hit, but the next thing I knew, the boat was on its side. I held Eric up as long as I could, but I lost my strength and he disappeared."

"Held him up?" I asked. "Couldn't he swim?"

"He wasn't much of a swimmer," Bill said. "Maybe he had some kind of a heart attack. We had just eaten two sandwiches when we went in the water."

By this time several boats were circling around us witnessing our only partially successful rescue operation.

One skipper brought his boat close aboard and yelled, "Can we help?"

I called back, "Perhaps you can take this man ashore while I continue to search."

He brought his boat alongside skillfully without touching us. Bill, after expressions of gratitude, jumped aboard.

We circled the area for another half hour and saw no sign of Eric. When we all agreed that further search was useless, I said, "Let's get some bearings on the spot so we can notify the Coast Guard." Charlie sighted across the compass on a house ashore with a distinctive pink roof and then took a cross bearing on the Matinicock Bell Buoy which was only a few

173

hundred yards away. After noting the compass bearings, we raised our sails and headed for our home port.

"I may be a coward," I said, "but I'm awfully glad that yawl came along and took Bill ashore. I'd surely have hated to explain to the other boy's parents why we failed to save their son."

Charlie said, "But can you imagine someone out sailing and not knowing how to swim?"

Jackie looked at him quizzically and replied, "No. It's hard to imagine."

"Jackie," I said, "You just have to learn no matter what."

But she never did.

The next day I wrote a letter to the commandant of the Coast Guard setting forth the bearings we had taken at the site and the facts surrounding the accident. The next day, too, Eric's father came to my office. We were ill at ease with each other. He was determined to be polite but the tenor of his questioning made it clear that he felt if we had arrived at the scene earlier, his son would not have been lost.

"You had some trouble starting your engine?" he asked.

I admitted the machine had been stubborn.

"If you had known what you now know about the need for prompt action, how much earlier could you have gotten there?" he continued.

"It's hard to say. Three or four minutes earlier, perhaps," I replied.

"Do you think if you had gotten there earlier, you might have saved him?" he asked.

"I don't know. I honestly don't know," I answered.

And to this day I still don't know. But I do know that I will never again take any longer than is absolutely necessary to assist another vessel.

15

Nearing Home Port

I once asked my doctor, who had been a frequent sailing companion, "When will I be too old to sail?"

His reply was, "The boat will tell you."

The boat has not yet told me in a commanding voice, but from time to time she whispers that we are homeward bound. I have used the same anchors for years; each year they grow a little heavier. Sails that originally were easy to raise or furl seem to have gained in area, and taking in a big genoa jib as *Shag* plows into a heavy head sea is a job for younger members of the crew.

There is no arbitrary age at which people grow too

old to enjoy sailing. I recall one afternoon, tacking down Penobscot Bay on *Skylark* in the hard afternoon southwester. My crew consisted of three men all in their vigorous middle years, and *Skylark* required their combined strength at each tack as she protested that she was overdressed for this particular party. Yet I knew that reducing sail would be even more onerous than carrying on. Ahead of us was a 35-foot sloop tacking down the same channel. As we drew nearer I could see that her crew was an elderly couple, certainly both in their seventies, with their abundant white hair flying in the increasing breeze. Curiously enough, they were not making nearly as rough going of it as we were. Unlike *Skylark*'s big jib that had to be winched in on each tack, the sloop had a self-trimming boom jib that changed sides with no one touching a line. As *Skylark* approached the narrow entrance to Pulpit Harbor, our destination, I turned on the engine, headed into the wind, and the crew furled the sails. Not so the sloop. Under full sail, the aging couple threaded the twisting entrance without moving from their seats. As we powered into the protected anchorage, we saw the sloop, still under sail, approach a dock. At exactly the proper distance, her skipper headed the sloop's bow into the wind and, sails aflutter, she came to a full stop right alongside the dock. At a leisurely pace, the lady left the cockpit, threw off the jib halyard from its cleat on the mast so the sail dropped to the deck, then stepped ashore with an already rigged bow line which she made fast to the dock.

"Neat but not gaudy?" I remarked evaluating this superlative performance.

"Jezol," one of my crew exclaimed in admiration. "Do you think we will be able to do that when we are their age?"

176

The Skipper in 1972.

"I don't know," I replied, "but I profoundly hope so."

The passage of time has disclosed to me the secret of this couple's competence. Experience and improved judgment substitute for waning physical strength. *Shag* has a self-tending jib for use in the trade winds, and while this smaller sail does not benefit her speed as would a large genoa, we are no longer racing and time is not all that important. Her big, powerful Barient winches make sail trimming comparatively effortless. While I would not care to invite a challenge to duplicate the performance of the sloop in Pulpit Harbor, *Shag* is equipped to do it just as easily if her skipper were as competent.

Take anchoring, for example. On *Skylark* nothing less that a 35-pound anchor satisfied me no matter how light the wind. On *Shag* we use a 19-pound, high tensile strength Danforth with a far lighter nylon line and let out more scope. Despite the fact that *Shag* is heavier than *Skylark,* I have been aboard when the smaller anchor remained firmly fixed in hurricane force winds. Furthermore, on *Skylark* we used to anchor with nearly total disregard for the depth. Now, with fathometer clicking, we search for the shallowest safe anchorage available in any chosen harbor. In addition, the engine is our ally when we depart an anchorage. Countless times I have watched the crew on other boats manfully haul their craft up to the anchor. It is fine exercise but a waste of strength. *Shag*'s powerful diesel engine propels her to a position over the anchor as the slack line is effortlessly brought aboard. When the anchor is directly beneath the bow, the line is made fast and the boat's momentum breaks the anchor out without expending an ounce of human energy.

A lifetime of observing the weather also helps in

hoarding strength. On earlier boats, virtually every shift in wind direction or speed dictated a change of sails. *Shag* leaves harbor in the morning conservatively dressed for her day's run. There seems little point in hoisting her lightest sails when the morning breeze is soft, because experience dictates that the sun's heat will fan the breeze into a fair blow by early afternoon. Perhaps we do not reach our destination in the shortest possible time, but what's the hurry? We now listen to the frequent official radio weather forecasts with an attention never lavished on them in earlier years. Along with everyone else we scoff at the frequent inaccuracy of these predictions, but the truth is that it is a rare occurrence when the weather bureau fails to predict a storm which might endanger small vessels. The bureau's errors are much more apt to be unnecessarily alarmist. I have come to believe that the small craft warnings are hoisted on every summer weekend and holiday, less as a prediction of things to come than as a brotherly bureaucratic gesture to the Coast Guard to keep the damn fool small boatmen from venturing forth.

For the last two summers I have hired young men of college age to perform those chores which have lost their glamour for me. Ray had completed his third year of college and was taking a year off before completing the course. David had completed preparatory school and was waiting a year before entering college. Both were good sailors and willing workers. Ray proved his worth early in the summer on a passage across the Bay of Fundy to the south coast of Nova Scotia. Just before we rounded Cape Sable, a predawn squall combined with vicious tide rips, dictated a reduction of sail. The big 180 degree genoa had been pulling like a workhorse through the night, but the time had come to shift to a far smaller sail. Ray, soaked to the skin by the icy water plunging over the bow, accomplished the shift in minimum time.

David had to wait longer in the second summer before I rediscovered the value of having the strength of youth available. Returning from New Brunswick, Canada, I ran afoul of a lobster pot while entering the little Maine harbor of Cutler. The line entwined in a Gordian knot around *Shag*'s propellor. After we anchored, I said, "Dave, this is where they separate the men from the boys, and you're the boys. Get your knife, dive in and clear the line." The water temperature was forty-eight degrees and David took fifteen minutes to saw through the coils before he emerged blue with cold. So far as I was concerned, he earned his whole summer's salary in that quarter of an hour.

Boys of college or school age are available for summer jobs of this kind. It makes a pleasant and profitable summer for the boys, and it takes a considerable load off a skipper past his prime.

So the end is not yet. I am hopeful that *Shag*'s lengthy log will have many more entries. There are still passages to be made, strange ports to visit, sunny days, and the occasional storm to be endured. Faithful performer that she has always been, I am confident that *Shag* will indeed tell me when the time comes to write:

THE END

Appendix

Faculty responsible for my education:

Rose—13 feet O class centerboard sloop, designed by John Alden, built by James Graves, Marblehead, Mass., sails by Cousen & Pratt. Owned 1923–1925.

Rose II—25 feet overall, 18 feet waterline, Triangle Class keel sloop, built by James Graves, sails by Cousen & Pratt. Owned 1926–1928.

Tarheel—30 feet overall, 25 feet waterline, gaff-rigged auxiliary sloop, designed and built by Casey, Fairhaven, Mass., sails by Manchester, engine: gasoline, 2 cylinder Kermath. Owned 1935–1938.

Rose—36 feet overall, 28 feet waterline, Marconi-rigged auxiliary cutter, designed by John Alden, built by Casey, sails by Ratsey, engine: gasoline, 4 cylinder 40 hp Gray. Owned 1938–1940.

Skylark—39 feet overall, 29 feet waterline, Marconi-rigged auxiliary yawl, designed and built by Casey, sails by Ratsey, engine: gasoline, 4 cylinder 40 hp Gray. Owned 1949–1967.

Shag—40 feet overall, 29 feet waterline, Marconi-rigged auxiliary fiberglass yawl, keel centerboard, designed by Wm. Tripp, built by Hinckley, Southwest Harbor, Maine, sails by Ratsey, engine: diesel Westerbeke, 4 cylinder 35 hp. Owned 1967–